LAST VOYAGE

LAST VOYAGE

SELECTED POEMS BY

Giovanni Pascoli

TRANSLATED BY

Deborah Brown, Richard Jackson
& Susan Thomas

Red Hen Press | Pasadena, CA

Last Voyage: Selected Poems
Translation copyright © 2010 by Deborah Brown,
Richard Jackson, & Susan Thomas

Book layout by Elizabeth Davis
Book design by Mark E. Cull

Pascoli, Giovanni, 1855 – 1912.
[Ultimo viaggio. English]
Last voyage : selected poems by Giovanni Pascoli / Giovanni Pascoli ;
translated by Deborah Brown, Richard Jackson & Susan Thomas.—1st ed.
    p. cm.
Includes bibliographical references.
ISBN 978-1-59709-487-0
I. Brown, Deborah. II. Jackson, Richard. III. Thomas, Susan. IV. Title.
PQ4726.P35U4813 2010
851'.8—dc22

The Annenberg Foundation, the California Arts Council, the James Irvine
Foundation, the Los Angeles County Arts Commission, the National
Endowment for the Arts, and Department of Cultural Affairs partially
support Red Hen Press.

First Edition

Published by Red Hen Press
Pasadena, CA
www.redhen.org

Acknowledgements

Some of the poems in this collection first appeared in the folliwing publications: *Center, A Journal of Literary Arts*: "O Vain Dream" (from "A Country Walk"); *Cold Mountain Review*: "The Dog", "November" (from "A Country Walk"); *Euphony*: "Ploughing", "Washerwomen", "Orphan" (from "A Country Walk"); *Diner*: "The Courtesan"; *Meridian Anthology of Contemporary Poetry*: "Thunderstorm"; *Northwest Review*: "Night-blooming Jasmine", "Passage", "The Clock at Barga"; *Potomac Review*: "The Beggar", "The Departure" (from "The Last Voyage"); *Smartish Pace*: "Autumn Diary", "Lightning", "November" and "Hens", "That Day", "The Railway" (from "A Country Walk").

Richard Jackson wishes to thank the Guggenheim Foundation, the University of Tennessee-Chattanooga Research Committee and the Council of Scholars for funding that enabled research on this project.

Deborah Brown wishes to thank the University of New Hampshire at Manchester for support that helped to make publication of this book possible.

Susan Thomas wishes to thank Jill Pralle and Giovanna Di Bernardo for their editorial assistance.

The translators wish to acknowledge the city of Barga, Italy; the Fondazione Giovanni Pascoli; and the curator and staff of the Museo di casa Pascoli in Castelvecchio (Barga), Italy, for their hospitality and continued interest in the work and life of Giovanni Pascoli.

TABLE OF CONTENTS

INTRODUCTION

In his preface to Myricae (1891), the young Pascoli (1855-1912) suggests that his early lyrics comprise an elegy for his father, an elegy that both laments his father's untimely death and asks forgiveness of him, and the reader: "They are like flapping of birds, rustling of cypresses, far singing of bells: they don't scorn a graveyard. For some tears, for sobbing, I hope to find forgiveness, since here less than elsewhere the reader will be able or will want to say: what do I care of your sorrow?" This dark tone, the rural images, the orientation around death, and indeed the colloquial texture of the verses themselves, prefigure Cesare Pavese. While Pascoli incorporated the hills around Barga, north of Lucca, into the texture and theme of his poems, Pavese used the hills around Santo Stefano Belbo, south of Torino, to do the same thing half a century later.

Born near Rimini, Pascoli was the product of a simple home, but one touched several times by death, including the assassination (never solved) of his father in 1867. He studied at the University of Bologna, where he later was professor of Italian literature.

He had begun writing early but did not publish a book until he was 36. From early on, his poems show a remarkable sense of linking everything into a kind of mysterious oneness where rocks and people, trees and animals all partake of the same essence. Overall, his philosophy might be characterized as a materialistic Platonism: indeed, an essay on "The Child" suggests that children, in resisting adult hierarchies, in taking an idealistically Platonic view of reality, arrive at the same mysterious essence his poems search for.

Pascoli's early poems owe something to the Romantic poet Leopardi (and to Wordsworth) in his desire to find a mysterious essence in the commonplace world. The poems are filled with precise observations, elemental images of rocks, country lanes, trees, flowers, birds, country churches, houses, and animals in a way that had not been seen before in Italian poetry, and which Pavese (and Montale) later developed even further. His style, often onomatopoetic, filled with sudden leaps, changes in point of view, non-standard grammar, and a penchant for the colon, all attempt to give a sense of the drama of the mind in the act of discovering itself. It often suggests the unconventional rhythms and language of Thomas Hardy. While all this illustrates a highly individual mind, and indeed a dramatic change in Italian poetry, Pascoli also saw in his country settings a tradition that offered safety and protection in a changing world.

As his poems developed, the specter of death seems to become more intense and overcomes a brief period of hope. For Pascoli, the very nature of poetry seems threatened. A number of analytic poems relating to artists and writers attest to his concern. The poems from the last part of his life, after he moves to Barga in 1895, struggle to make sense of this deteriorating world. Elegiac narrative tends to replace elegiac lyric as the complex world he describes tends to burst the lyric's seams.

In this last period, on which the second half of this selection focuses, Pascoli makes use of his considerable classical learning. (He wrote a number of eloquent poems in Latin). The Banquet Songs (1904) suggest a Greek or Roman setting, but a setting that Pascoli completely transforms for he is not interested, finally, in recording the past or even revisiting it, but in absorbing it into the fabric of his own life. The poems, especially the poems of "The Last Voyage," provide him an opportunity to voice his own concerns through the character of Ulysses as he, as in Tennyson's famous poem, sets out on his last assigned voyage to bury Poseidon's oar far from land. Ulysses, retracing his famous first voyage in The Odyssey, becomes an image for Pascoli's own retreat into his past to evaluate his triumphs and his mistakes. (Again, something Pavese will do with his own invented characters.)

The translation of these poems was a group project: one of the three of us would offer a rough version that the others would then 'workshop' and critique until a second, third, and fourth draft were done. In the end, these 'final' versions were checked and smoothed. In all, we followed Samuel Johnson's dictum that a translation must first of all be good in its "target language." As a result, some good poems in Italian were left out because they did the same things as other poems, or they didn't sound as good in English. As a whole we tried to follow the general form and stanzaic patterns of the poems, especially when line breaks seemed crucial. In some places, we have used italics for clarity.

For this selection, we have included in the first section some brief lyrics followed by several longer lyrics, several of them taken from sectioned poems but including one long representative sequence, "A Country Walk." The second section includes three longer poems, generally narrative in nature, one of which is quite formal ("The Sleep of Odysseus"). The last section is Pascoli's imaginative return journey back through the Odyssey with an aging Odysseus, (an idea borrowed from Tennyson and Dante). We feel that this gives a good introductory sense of the range and evolution of Pascoli's style and concerns.

While Pascoli was a prolific writer, also publishing many Latin poems, we have taken our selections from Myricae (1891), Primi Poemetti (1897), Canti di Castelvecchio (1903) and Poemi Conviviali (1904).

RJ

I
Lyrics

Novembre

Gemmea l'aria, il sole così chiaro
che tu ricerchi gli albicocchi in fiore,
e del prunalbo l'odorino amaro
         senti nel cuore

Ma secco è il pruno, e le stecchite piante
di nere trame segnano il sereno,
e vuoto il cielo, e cavo al piè sonante
         sembra il terreno.

Silenzio, intorno: solo, alle ventate,
odi lontano, da giardini ed orti,
di foglie un cader fragile. È l'estate,
         fredda, dei morti.

November

The jeweled air: the clear sun:
you look for the flowering apricot tree,
and smell the bitter scent of hawthorn
                    in your heart.

But the thorn has dried out, and skeletal plants
weave black threads into the clear blue sky,
into the empty vault of heaven, and the hollow earth
                    rings with every footstep.

Silence, all around: from far away you hear
only the gusting of the wind, and from the orchards
and gardens, the fragile descent of leaves. It is
                    the cold summer of the dead.

Il Lampo

E cielo e terra si mostrò qual era:

la terra ansante, livida, in sussulto;
il cielo ingombro, tragico, disfatto:
bianca bianca nel tacito tumulto
una casa apparì sparì d'un tratto;
come un occhio, che, largo, esterrefatto,
s'aprì si chiuse, nella notte nera.

Lightning

And the sky and the earth showed this sight:

the earth gray, bruised, quivering;
the sky shadowy, tragic, falling apart:
suddenly, white in the mute confusion, shining,
a house appeared for a moment then departed;
like an eye, opened wide in fright, startled,
opened then closed, in the black night.

DIARIO AUTUNNALE

Bologna, 2 novembre.

Per il viale, neri lunghi stormi,
facendo tutto a man a man più fosco,
passano: preti, nella nebbia informi,
che vanno in riga a San Michele in Bosco.

Vanno. Tra loro parlano di morte.
Cadono sopra loro foglie morte.

Sono con loro morte foglie sole.
Vanno a guardare l'agonia del sole.

Autumn Diary

Along the avenue, long black flocks
make everything gloomy little by little.
They pass: priests in their shapeless cassocks
go in a rigid line to St. Michele in Bosco.

They go. They speak of death among themselves.
Above them, dead leaves are falling.

I am with them among the sunny dying leaves.
They go to watch over the agony of the sun.

Il Gelsomino Notturno

E s'aprono i fiori notturni,
nell'ora che penso a' miei cari.
Sono apparse in mezzo ai viburni
le farfalle crepuscolari.
Da un pezzo si tacquero i gridi:
là sola una casa bisbiglia.
Sotto l'ali dormono i nidi,
come gli occhi sotto le ciglia.
Dai calici aperti si esala
l'odore di fragole rosse.
Splende un lume là nella sala.
Nasce l'erba sopra le fosse.
Un'ape tardiva sussurra
trovando già prese le celle.
La Chioccetta per l'aia azzurra
va col suo pigolìo di stelle.
Per tutta la notte s'esala
l'odore che passa col vento.
Passa il lume su per la scala;
brilla al primo piano: s'è spento . . .
E' l'alba: si chiudono i petali
un poco gualciti; si cova,
dentro l'urna molle e segreta,
non so che felicità nuova.

Night-blooming Jasmine

And the night-blooming flowers open,
open in the same hour I remember those I love.
In the middle of the viburnums
the twilight butterflies have appeared.

After a while all noise will quiet.
There, only a house is whispering.
Nests sleep under wings,
like eyes under eyelashes.

Open goblets exhale
the perfume of strawberries.
A light shines there in the room,
grass sprouts over the graves.

A late bee buzzes at the hive
finding all the cells taken.
The Hen runs through the sky's blue
yard to the chirping of stars.

The whole night exhales
a scent that disappears in the wind.
A light ascends the stairs;
it shines on the second floor: goes out.

And then dawn: the petals close
a little crumpled. Something soft
and secret is brooding in an urn,
some new happiness I can't understand yet.

TEMPORALE

E' mezzodì. Rintomba.
Tacciono le cicale
nelle stridule seccie.
E chiaro un tuon rimbomba
dopo uno stanco, uguale,
rotolare di breccie.
Rondini ad ali aperte
fanno echeggiar la loggia
de' lor piccoli scoppi.
Già, dopo l'afa inerte,
fanno rumor di pioggia
le fogline dei pioppi.
Un tuon sgretola l'aria.
Sembra venuto sera.
Picchia ogni anta su l'anta.
Serrano. Solitaria
s'ode una capinera,
là, che canta... che canta . . .
E l'acqua cade, a grosse
goccie, poi giù a torrenti,
sopra i fumidi campi.
S'è sfatto il cielo: a scosse
v'entrano urlando i venti
e vi sbisciano i lampi.

Thunderstorm

Noon. The thunder peals.
Cicadas quiet in the shrill
fields of stubble.

A deep boom of thunder
after the dull, even rolling
of worn-down stones.

Swallows with open wings
echo on the balcony
with little bursts of sound.

A thunderclap shatters the air.
It seems that night has come.
Every shutter knocks against

another shutter. They close.
Only a blackbird is heard there,
singing, singing.

Water falls in heavy
drops, then torrents fall
into the steaming fields.

The sky is exhausted; by fits
and starts the winds come shrieking,
and make the lamps flicker.

Cresce in un gran sussulto
l'acqua, dopo ogni rotto
schianto ch'aspro diroccia;
mentre, col suo singulto
trepido, passa sotto
l'acquazzone una chioccia.
Appena tace il tuono,
che quando al fin già pare,
fa tremare ogni vetro,
tra il vento e l'acqua, buono,
s'ode quel croccolare
co' suoi pigolìi dietro.

Water rises in a great leap
then crashes hard, as in a fall
from a great height,

while with a trembling cackle
a hen disappears
into the great downpour.

Scarcely has the thunder quieted,
and the end already come, when
all the windows tremble again.

But—good—the hen's cackling
sounds through all the wind and water,
and, behind it, another fainter sound.

Il Transito

Il cigno canta. In mezzo delle lame
rombano le sue voci lunghe e chiare,
come percossi cembali di rame.

È l'infinita tenebra polare.
Grandi montagne d'un eterno gelo
póntano sopra il lastrico del mare.

Il cigno canta; e lentamente il cielo
sfuma nel buio, e si colora in giallo;
spunta una luce verde a stelo a stelo.

Come arpe qua e là tocche, il metallo
di quella voce tìntina; già sfiora
la verde luce i picchi di cristallo.

E nella notte, che ne trascolora,
un immenso iridato arco sfavilla,
e i portici profondi apre l'aurora.

L'arco verde e vermiglio arde, zampilla,
a frecce, a fasci; e poi palpita, frana
tacitamente, e riascende e brilla.

Col suono d'un rintocco di campana
che squilli ultimo, il cigno agita l'ale:
l'ale grandi grandi apre, e s'allontana

candido, nella luce boreale.

Passage

The swan sings. From deep in the marshes,
its voice chimes sharp and clear
like the striking of copper cymbals.

This is the endless polar darkness.
Great mountains of eternal frost
lean against the ice plates of the ocean.

The swan sings; and slowly the sky
fades into the darkness and tints itself yellow.
A green light rises from star to star.

The swan's metal voice rings like a harp
caressed here and there; already the green
northern lights glaze the icy mountain peaks.

And in the deepening night,
an immense iridescent arc grows
into huge ladders that spread open the aurora.

The green and vermillion glow catches fire,
shoots rays, pulsates, subsides, rises again,
exploding, all in utter silence.

With a sound like the bell's final
angelus chime, the swan shakes its wings:
the wings open, and lift, enormous,

pure white, into the boreal night.

Il Libro

I

Sopra il leggìo di quercia è nell'altana,
aperto, il libro. Quella quercia ancora,
esercitata dalla tramontana,

viveva nella sua selva sonora;
e quel libro era antico. Eccolo: aperto,
sembra che ascolti il tarlo che lavora.

E sembra ch'uno (donde mai? non, certo,
dal tremulo uscio, cui tentenna il vento
delle montagne e il vento del deserto,

sorti d'un tratto . . .) sia venuto, e lento
sfogli - se n'ode il crepitar leggiero -
le carte. E l'uomo non vedo io: lo sento,
invisibile, là, come il pensiero . . .

II

Un uomo è là, che sfoglia dalla prima
carta all'estrema, rapido, e pian piano
va, dall'estrema, a ritrovar la prima.

E poi nell'ira del cercar suo vano
volta i fragili fogli a venti, a trenta,
a cento, con l'impazïente mano.

THE BOOK

I

The oak bookstand on the terrace, and on it,
open, the book. The oak tested
by the north wind, that lived

inside the sounds of the forests;
and that book from a bygone time. Look at it:
open, there seems to be the sound of a woodworm at work.

And the sound seems (but from where? not, surely,
from the moving door, wavering in the wind
from the mountain, and the wind from the desert,

by turns . . .) slowly coming and going,
rustling—unless it's the slight crackling
of papers. And the man I don't see: I sense him,
barely perceptible, there, like a thought.

II

A man is there, leafing from the opening pages
to the last, quickly, and then, very slowly,
going to the end to find the beginning again.

And then, angry at searching in vain,
he turns the delicate pages from twenty, to thirty,
to a hundred with an impatient hand.

E poi li volge a uno a uno, lenta-
mente, esitando; ma via via più forte,
più presto, i fogli contro i fogli avventa.

Sosta... Trovò? Non gemono le porte
più, tutto oscilla in un silenzio austero.
Legge?... Un istante; e volta le contorte

pagine, e torna ad inseguire il vero.

III

E sfoglia ancora; al vespro, che da nere
nubi rosseggia; tra un errar di tuoni,
tra un alïare come di chimere.

E sfoglia ancora, mentre i padiglioni
tumidi al vento l'ombra tende, e viene
con le deserte costellazïoni

la sacra notte. Ancora e sempre: bene
io n'odo il crepito arido tra canti
lunghi nel cielo come di sirene.

Sempre. Io lo sento, tra le voci erranti,
invisibile, là, come il pensiero,
che sfoglia, avanti indietro, indietro avanti,

sotto le stelle, il libro del mistero.

And then he turns them one by one, slowly
hesitating; but gradually with more force
more quickly, he slaps page against page.

Stop. What does he find? The door's not groaning,
not swinging back and forth in the painful silence.
Is he reading? For an instant, yes; then turns away from

the crumpled page, and returns to a search for truth.

III

And still he turns pages; at evening, the dark
clouds redden; between them, thunder rolls,
and a ghost-like fluttering.

And still he turns the pages, while shadows
stretch out like tents swollen by the wind,
stretching toward a deserted constellation

in the sacred night. Always the same:
I never hear the dry rustling between
the siren songs drawn out through the sky.

Always. I feel them, in roaming voices,
invisible, there, like the thought,
turning, back and forth, back and forth,

under the stars, the book of mystery.

IL BACIO DEL MORTO

I

È tacito, è grigio il mattino;
la terra ha un odore di funghi;
di gocciole è pieno il giardino.

Immobili tra la leggiera
caligine gli alberi: lunghi
lamenti di vaporïera.

I solchi ho nel cuore, i sussulti,
d'un pianto sognato: parole,
sospiri avanzati ai singulti:

un solco sul labbro, che duole.

II

Chi sei, che venisti, coi lieti
tuoi passi, da me nella notte?
Non so; non ricordo: piangevi.

Piangevi: io sentii per il viso
mio piangere fredde, dirotte,
le stille dall'occhio tuo fiso

THE KISS OF DEATH

I

The morning is silent, gray;
the earth smells like mushrooms;
the whole garden is dripping.

The trees are still
against the haze: long
wailing of a steam engine.

The tracks run through my heart, shudders
from mournful dreams: words, sighs
left over from my solitary nest of sleep:

and a track down my lip: that grief.

II

Who are you that came with rising
footsteps, came to me in the night?
I don't know; don't remember: I was weeping.

I was weeping: I saw your face
my cold tears pouring down,
the steady dripping from your eyes

su me: io sentii che accostavi
le labbra al mio labbro a baciarmi;
e invano volli io levar gravi

le palpebre: gravi: due marmi.

III

Chi sei? donde vieni? presente
tuttora? mi vedi? mi sai?
e lacrimi tacitamente?

Chi sei ? Trema ancora la porta.
Certo eri di quelli che amai,
ma forse non so che sei morta . . .

Né so come un'ombra d'arcano,
tra l'umida nebbia leggiera,
io senta in quel lungo lontano
saluto di vaporiera.

onto me: I felt your mouth approaching
to kiss me on the lip
and you wished in vain for the raising of

my heavy eyelids: heavy: two marbles.

III

Who are you? Where do you come from? Are you
still here? Do you see me? Do you know me?
And those silent tears?

Who are you? Again the door is trembling.
Certainly you come from someone I loved,
but perhaps I don't know you are dead.

Nor do I know, in the shadow of mystery,
among the thin mists, how
I can hear from such a distance,
the farewell of a steam engine.

L'ora Di Barga

Al mio cantuccio, donde non sento
se non le reste brusir del grano,
il suon dell'ore viene col vento
dal non veduto borgo montano:
suono che uguale, che blando cade,
come una voce che persuade.
Tu dici, E` l'ora; tu dici, E` tardi,
voce che cadi blanda dal cielo.
Ma un poco ancora lascia che guardi
l'albero, il ragno, l'ape, lo stelo,
cose ch'han molti secoli o un anno
o un'ora, e quelle nubi che vanno.
Lasciami immoto qui rimanere
fra tanto moto d'ale e di fronde;
e udire il gallo che da un podere
chiama, e da un altro l'altro risponde,
e, quando altrove l'anima è fissa,
gli strilli d'una cincia che rissa.
E suona ancora l'ora, e mi manda
prima un suo grido di meraviglia
tinnulo, e quindi con la sua blanda
voce di prima parla e consiglia,
e grave grave grave m'incuora:
mi dice, E` tardi; mi dice, E` l'ora.

The Clock at Barga

In my corner, where I hear nothing
but the rustling of the bearded grain,
wind brings the striking of the clock
from the unseen mountain village above:
a sound that falls evenly, softly,
like a persuading voice.

You say, *It is time*; you say *It is late*,
voice that falls softly from the sky:
But let me look a little longer
at the tree, the spider, the bees, the stem,
things that have centuries in them, or a year
or an hour, and those clouds that are passing.

Let me stay here motionless
near so much movement of wings and leaves;
and listen to the rooster calling from one farm,
hear another rooster answer from another farm;
and, when the soul's attention is elsewhere,
the squeaking of a titmouse taking flight.

And the hour sounds again, and speaks to me
first with a tinkling cry of wonder, and then
afterwards, with its original mild
voice, it speaks and counsels
gravely, gravely, it encourages me:
it tells me, *It is late*, it tells me, *It is time*.

Tu vuoi che pensi dunque al ritorno,
voce che cadi blanda dal cielo!
Ma bello è questo poco di giorno
che mi traluce come da un velo!
Lo so ch'è l'ora, lo so ch'è tardi;
ma un poco ancora lascia che guardi.
Lascia che guardi dentro il mio cuore,
lascia ch'io viva del mio passato;
se c'è sul bronco sempre quel fiore,
s'io trovi un bacio che non ho dato!
Nel mio cantuccio d'ombra romita
lascia ch'io pianga su la mia vita!
E suona ancora l'ora, e mi squilla
due volte un grido quasi di cruccio,
e poi, tornata blanda e tranquilla,
mi persuade nel mio cantuccio:
è tardi! è l'ora! Sì, ritorniamo
dove son quelli ch'amano ed amo.

You want me to think, then, of returning,
voice that falls mildly from heaven.
But, how beautiful is this small part of the day
which shines through me like a veil!
I know it is time, I know it is late;
but let me stay a little longer to watch.

Let me see inside my heart,
let me live inside my past.
There may be a flower still blooming on a tree-stump,
I may find a kiss not yet given:
in my lonely spot of shade,
let me weep over my life.

And again the hour sounds, and twice
I am shaken by a cry almost of annoyance,
and then it turns soft and mild,
persuading me into my corner:
It is late! It is time! Yes, let me go back where
there are those who love and those whom I love.

L'ULTIMA PASSEGGIATA

I. *Arano*

Al campo, dove roggio nel filare
qualche pampano brilla, e dalle fratte
sembra la nebbia mattinal fumare,

arano: a lente grida, uno le lente
vacche spinge; altri semina; un ribatte
le porche con sua marra pazïente;

ché il passero saputo in cor già gode,
e il tutto spia dai rami irti del moro;
e il pettirosso: nelle siepi s'ode
il suo sottil tintinno come d'oro.

II. *Di lassù*

La lodola perduta nell'aurora
si spazia, e di lassù canta alla villa,
che un fil di fumo qua e là vapora;

di lassù largamente bruni farsi
i solchi mira quella sua pupilla
lontana, e i bianchi bovi a coppie sparsi.

Qualche zolla nel campo umido e nero
luccica al sole, netta come specchio:
fa il villano mannelle in suo pensiero,
e il canto del cuculo ha nell'orecchio.

A Country Walk

I. *Plowing*

In the field, where rows of vines have turned red,
some grape leaves sparkle and the underbrush
seems to smoke in the morning mist,

they're plowing: someone screams to slow down,
one of the sluggish cows pushes; the others scatter;
somebody tends the ridges with a patient hoe;

so the sly sparrow and the other spies of the branches,
have already feasted in their hearts on the berries;
and the robin: deep in the hedgerows he hears
his own fine voice like tinkling gold.

II. *From Above*

The lark is lost in the spaces of dawn
so he sings from above to the houses,
a thread of smoke fading here and there.

From above, his pupils widen,
the furrows have a burnished design.
From that far the white dots of cows lie scattered.

In the field, dark, damp clods of earth
glitter in the sun, clear as a mirror:
but the farmer works deep in thought
and in his ear holds the song of the cuckoo.

III. *Galline*

Al cader delle foglie, alla massaia
non piange il vecchio cor, come a noi grami:
che d'arguti galletti ha piena l'aia;

e spessi nella pace del mattino
delle utili galline ode i richiami:
zeppo, il granaio; il vin canta nel tino.

Cantano a sera intorno a lei stornelli
le fiorenti ragazze occhi pensosi,
mentre il granturco sfogliano, e i monelli
ruzzano nei cartocci strepitosi.

IV. *Lavandare*

Nel campo mezzo grigio e mezzo nero
resta un aratro senza buoi che pare
dimenticato, tra il vapor leggero.

E cadenzato dalla gora viene
lo sciabordare delle lavandare
con tonfi spessi e lunghe cantilene:

Il vento soffia e nevica la frasca,
e tu non torni ancora al tuo paese!
quando partisti, come son rimasta!
come l'aratro in mezzo alla maggese.

III. *Hens*

When the leaves fall, the housewife
doesn't grieve in her heart, as we grieve;
the shrillness of the cocks fills the air;

often through the peace of the morning
she hears the calls of her laying hens.
It's crammed, the granary; wine sings in the vats.

They sing their folksongs through the night,
those young girls with their pensive eyes
while they shuck corn, and the devilish
cocks prance deafeningly in the sheaves.

IV. *Two Children*

The two children stand up: one boy, with difficulty,
he is numb; the other, solemn. The first one
raises his harvest basket slowly;

and into the other's basket lets fall, carefully,
his winnings, chips of dung for burning.
The winner walks away more proud than burdened.

The vanquished boy sits, tries another time
with hazel nuts, spreads them, gathers them again,
and cries out that he has no luck!

V. *I due bimbi*

I due bimbi si rizzano: uno, a stento,
indolenzito; grave, l'altro: il primo
alza il corbello con un gesto lento;

e in quel dell'altro fa cader, bel bello,
il suo tesoro d'accattato fimo:
e quello va più carico e più snello.

Il vinto siede, prova un'altra volta
coi noccioli, li sperpera, li aduna,
e dice (forse al grande olmo che ascolta?):
E poi si dica che non ha fortuna!

VI. *La via ferrata*

Tra gli argini su cui mucche tranquilla-
mente pascono, bruna si difila
la via ferrata che lontano brilla;

e nel cielo di perla dritti, uguali,
con loro trama delle aeree fila
digradano in fuggente ordine i pali.

Qual di gemiti e d'ululi rombando
cresce e dilegua femminil lamento?
I fili di metallo a quando a quando
squillano, immensa arpa sonora, al vento.

V. *The Washerwomen*

In a field half-gray, half-black,
stands a plow without oxen, that seems
forgotten among light autumn mists.

And from the millstream comes
the rhythmic sounds of washerwomen—
frequent splashing and endless refrains:

The wind blows white on the bush,
and still you don't come home!
As you left so have I stayed on!
Like a plow in a fallow field.

VI. *The Railway*

Between the embankments where cows calmly
graze, railroad ties line up in brown rows
while the rails gleam into the distance

and the telegraph poles stand upright, equal,
weaving their threads of air in descending
order into the pearly sky above.

What groans and shrieking howls rise
then dwindle in almost feminine lament!
The metal wires ring from time to time,
an immense harp playing in the wind.

VII. *Festa lontana*

Un piccolo infinito scampando
ne ronza e vibra, come d'una festa
assai lontana, dietro un vel d'oblio.

Là, quando ondando vanno le campane,
scoprono i vecchi per la via la testa
bianca, e lo sguardo al suoi fisso rimane.

Ma tondi gli occhi sgranano i bimbetti,
cui trema intorno il loro ciel sereno.
Strillano al crepitar de' mortaretti.
Mamma li stringe all'odorato seno.

VIII. *Quel giorno*

Dopo rissosi cinguettìi nell'aria,
le rondini lasciato hanno i veroni
della Cura fra gli olmi solitaria.

Quanti quel roseo campanil bisbigli
udì, quel giorno, o strilli di rondoni
impazïenti a gl'inquïeti figli!

Or nel silenzio del meriggio urtare
là dentro odo una seggiola, una gonna
frusciar d'un tratto: alla finestra appare
curïoso un gentil viso di donna.

VII. *Distant Country Fair*

The endless chiming of distant bells
which strike and hum, as from a distant
country fair, recalls layers of memory.

The surge of that chiming brings
out the town elders, who know the way
even with their eyes fixed on the ground.

But the children's eyes grow round in
wonder as they shiver in the clear evening.
They shriek at the boom of firecrackers
as mothers clasp them tight to their breasts.

VIII. *That Day*

After screeching skirmishes in the air
the swallows have left the terraced roofs
of the lonely churchyard under the elms.

How much whispering the pink bell tower
heard that day—oh, the shrieks of the swallows
impatient with their restless young.

Within the silence of the noon hour's chime,
in the tower the sudden rustling of a skirt
against a chair: at the window appears
the curious tender face of a woman.

IX. *Mezzogiorno*

L'osteria della Pergola è in faccende:
piena è di grida, di brusio, di sordi
tonfi; il camin fumante a tratti splende.

Sulla soglia, tra il nembo degli odori
pingui, un mendico brontola: Altri tordi
c'era una volta, e altri cacciatori.

Dice, e il cor s'è beato. Mezzogiorno
dal villaggio a rintocchi lenti squilla;
e dai remoti campanili intorno
un'ondata di riso empie la villa.

X. *Già dalla mattina*

Acqua, rimbomba; dondola, cassetta;
gira, coperchio, intorno la bronzina;
versa, tramoggia, il gran dalla bocchetta;

spolvero, svola. Nero da una fratta
l'asino attende già dalla mattina
presso la risonante cateratta.

Le orecchie scrolla e volgesi a guardare
ché tardi, tra finire, andar bel bello,
intridere, spianare ed infornare,
sul desco fumerai, pan di cruschello.

IX. *Noontime*

The bar under the trellis is busy:
Full of screams, shouts, deafening thumps.
From time to time, puffs of smoke from the fire.

On the threshold, within range of the odors
of fat, a beggar mumbles: once upon a time
there were other hunters, other fools.

He says this, but his heart is happy.
Noontime in the village: the slow
tolling from the distant bell towers
and a wave of laughter fills the village.

X. *Already in the Early Morning*

Water, booming; the collecting box swings
round; the lid turns around a bearing;
grain pours out from the tiny opening;

flour flies. The black donkey already
waits in the early morning on the thorny
hillside near the rushing cascade.

His ears twitch and he turns to see,
later, in the midst of the gradual finishing up,
the kneading, the leveling and baking,
steam rising from the table, whole wheat bread.

XI. *Carrettiere*

O carrettiere che dai neri monti
vieni tranquillo, e fosti nella notte
sotto ardue rupi, sopra aerei ponti;

che mai diceva il querulo aquilone
che muggia nelle forre e fra le grotte?
Ma tu dormivi sopra il tuo carbone.

A mano a mano lungo lo stradale
venìa fischiando un soffio di procella:
ma tu sognavi ch'era di natale;
udivi i suoni d'una cennamella.

XII. *In capannello*

Cigola il lungo e tremulo cancello
la via sbarra: ritte allo steccato
cianciano le comari in capannello:

parlan d'uno ch'è un altro scrivo scrivo;
del vin che costa un occhio, e ce n'è stato;
del governo; di questo mal cattivo;

del piccino; del grande ch'è sui venti;
del maiale, che mangia e non ingrassa -
Nero avanti a quelli occhi indifferenti
il traino con fragore di tuon passa.

XI. *The Cart Driver*

Driver, who came from the black mountains,
slowly, and traveled in the night
below steep cliffs and over bridges in the air;

the fierce north wind that roars in ravines
and caves never stopped you?
And you slept right over your coal.

From time to time along the way
the breath of a storm whistled an apology:
but you dreamed you were at home;
you heard the sounds of a bagpipe.

XII. *The Bell*

Along its whole length, the gate squeaks
and trembles and blocks the street. Standing
there, a group of old women gossip:

speaking of one thing or another, of this and that;
of the wine which costs an eye and isn't good;
of the government; of everything that is wrong;

of the little children; of the grownup child who is
twenty;
of the pigs which eat but don't fatten.
Right in front of their eyes, a black train
passes, indifferent, rumbling like thunder.

XIII. *Il cane*

Noi mentre il mondo va per la sua strada,
noi ci rodiamo, e in cuor doppio è l'affanno,
e perchè vada, e perchè lento vada.

Tal, quando passa il grave carro avanti
del casolare, che il rozzon normanno
stampa il suolo con zoccoli sonanti,

sbuca il can dalla fratta, come il vento;
lo precorre, rincorre; uggiola, abbaia.
Il carro è dilungato lento lento.
Il cane torna sternutando all'aia.

XIV. *O reginella*

Non trasandata ti creò per vero
la cara madre: tal, lungo la via,
tela albeggia, onde godi in tuo pensiero:

presso è la festa, e ognuno a te domanda
candidi i lini, poi che in tua balìa
è il cassone odorato di lavanda.

Felici i vecchi tuoi; felici ancora
i tuoi fratelli; e più, quando a te piaccia,
chi sua ti porti nella sua dimora,
o reginella dalle bianche braccia.

XIII. *The Dog*

While the world goes by his street
we fret, our hearts beat double because
he goes there, and because he goes there slowly.

When the heavy carriage passes in front
of the cottage, the poor old Norman horse
stamps the ground with ringing hoofs,

the dog pops out of the brake like the wind;
he chases, runs in front, barks, whines.
The carriage goes by slowly, slowly.
The dog turns back, snorting, to the farmyard.

XIV. *O Little Queen*

Truly, your dear mother has not failed to prepare
you: so that, after a while, you have such white
linens, such waves of pleasure in your thoughts:

the feast day is close and everyone asks you
for fresh white linen, which is in your care
resting in a lavender-scented chest.

How happy to be your parents; happy also
your brothers: and even more, when it pleases you,
your husband, when he brings you home,
O little beauty with the white arms.

XV. *Ti chiama*

Quella sera i tuoi vecchi (odi? ti chiama
la cara madre: al fumo della bruna
pentola, con irrequieta brama,

rissano i bimbi: frena tu, severa,
quinci una mano trepida, quindi una
stridula bocca, e al piccol volgo impera;

sì che in pace, tra un grande acciottolìo,
bruchi la sussurrante famigliola),
quella notte i tuoi vecchi un dolor pio
soffocheranno contro le lenzuola.

XVI. *O vano sogno*

Al camino, ove scoppia la mortella
tra la stipa, o ch'io sogno, o veglio teco:
mangio teco radicchio e pimpinella.

Al soffiar delle raffiche sonanti,
l'aulente fieno sul forcon m'arreco,
e visito i miei dolci ruminanti:

XV. *She Calls You*

That evening the old people—when
the blackened pot boils, do you smell it?
When your mother calls you, she wants you

there, with the brawling children. But you,
you hold back; there are her fluttering hands,
her sharp mouth, and the way she rules the children.

she's at peace, in the grand clatter,
with the noises of the family supper.
That night the old devout people suffer,
a sorrow they press against their sheets.

XVI. *O Vain Dream*

By the fireplace where the myrtle bursts in the
brush wood, let me dream, let me sit up
eating winter chicory and burnet.

At the first gust of shrieking gales,
I rush out to visit my gentle herd,
bringing fragrant hay on my pitchfork.

poi salgo, e teco - O vano sogno! Quando
nella macchia fiorisce il pan porcino,
lo scolaro i suoi divi ozi lasciando
spolvera il badïale calepino:

chioccola il merlo, fischia il beccaccino;
anch'io torno a cantare in mio latino.

But then I go upstairs to you, O vain dream!
When in the woods, the cyclamen flowers,
I drain off their marvelous liquid,
leaving fine dust for an ample lexicon:

The blackbird trills, the snipe whistles;
and I, too, return to sing in my own language.

X Agosto

San Lorenzo, io lo so perché tanto
di stelle per l'aria tranquilla
arde e cade, perché sì gran pianto
nel concavo cielo sfavilla.

Ritornava una rondine al tetto:
l'uccisero: cadde tra spini:
ella aveva nel becco un insetto:
la cena de' suoi rondinini.

Ora è là come in croce, che tende
quel verme a quel cielo lontano;
e il suo nido è nell'ombra, che attende,
che pigola sempre più piano.

Anche un uomo tornava al suo nido:
l'uccisero: disse: Perdono;
e restò negli aperti occhi un grido
portava due bambole in dono . . .

Ora là, nella casa romita,
lo aspettano, aspettano in vano:
egli immobile, attonito, addita
le bambole al cielo lontano

E tu, Cielo, dall'alto dei mondi
sereni, infinito, immortale,
Oh! d'un pianto di stelle lo inondi
quest'atomo opaco del Male!

AUGUST 10 (FROM ELEGIES, III)

St. Lorenzo, I know why so many
stars are burning and falling
through the tranquil air, why they
weep under the hollow sparkling sky.

A swallow, returning to the roof,
was killed. It fell into thorns:
in its beak, it held an insect,
dinner for its young.

He lies there now, as though crucified,
holding the maggot up to the faraway sky;
and his young, they wait, their nest now
in shadow, their chirping softer and softer.

A man, too, was returning to the nest:
They killed him: he said: I am lost;
and a scream remained in his open eyes:
he was carrying two dolls as presents.

Now, in the empty house
they wait for him, they wait in vain:
he is motionless, astonished, he points
the dolls toward the distant sky.

And you, Sky, from your height above
the world, serene, infinite, immortal.
Oh! The stars are flooded with grief
at this world—impenetrable atom of Evil.

II

Narrative Poems

L'etèra

O quale, un'alba, Myrrhine si spense,
la molto cara, quando ancor si spense
stanca l'insonne lampada lasciva,
conscia di tutto. Ma v'infuse Evèno
ancor rugiada di perenne ulivo;
e su la via dei campi in un tempietto,
chiuso, di marmo, appese la lucerna
che rischiarasse a Myrrhine le notti;
in vano: ch'ella alfin dormiva, e sola.
Ma lievemente a quel chiarore, ardente
nel gran silenzio opaco della strada,
volò, con lo stridìo d'una falena,
l'anima d'essa: ché vagava in cerca
del corpo amato, per vederlo a cora,
bianco, perfetto, il suo bel fior di carne,
fiore che apriva tutta la corolla
tutta la notte, e si chiudea su l'alba
avido ed aspro, senza più profumo.
Or la falena stridula cercava
quel morto fiore, e batté l'ali al lume
della lucerna, che sapea gli amori;
ma il corpo amato ella non vide, chiuso,
coi molti arcani balsami, nell'arca.

Né volle andare al suo cammino ancora
come le aeree anime, cui tarda
prendere il volo, simili all'incenso
il cui destino è d'olezzar vanendo.

The Courtesan

This is how one dawn Myrrhine extinguished
herself, the best loved of all courtesans, and
how the lamp extinguished itself as well,
the sleepless, exhausted lascivious lamp,
which saw all and knew all that went on.
But Evanus had already filled the lamp
with olive oil; and in a locked marble temple
by the side of the road skirting the fields,
hung the lantern that brightened Myrrhine's
nights, and in vain, for she was asleep at
last and alone. But in some glimmer of
light that burned in the dark silence of
the street, with a whirr like a moth's, flew
her spirit, which wandered in search of its
own body, to see it again, perfect, white,
in its prime, like a flower that opens at night,
then closes at dawn, harsh and greedy,
without a scent. Just now, the moth was
searching for some dead flower and beat
its wings in the flame of the lamp that watched
over the lovers; but it didn't know its own body
closed in the casket, so changed, with so many
mysterious balms of the grave.

She didn't want to make this journey
again with the spirits of the air; which
take flight, like incense that is destined
to fade as quickly as it scents the air.

E per l'opaca strada ecco sorvenne
un coro allegro, con le faci spente,
da un giovenile florido banchetto.
E Moscho a quella lampada solinga
la teda accese, e lesse nella stele:
MYRRHINE AL LUME DELLA SUA LUCERNA
DORME. È LA PRIMA VOLTA ORA, E PER SEMPRE.
E disse: Amici, buona a noi la sorte!
Myrrhine dorme le sue notti, e sola!
Io ben pregava Amore iddio, che al fine
m'addormentasse Myrrhine nel cuore:
pregai l'Amore e m'ascoltò la Morte.
E Callia disse: Ell'era un'ape, e il miele
stillava, ma pungea col pungiglione.
E disse Agathia: Ella mesceva ai bocci
d'amor le spine, ai dolci fichi i funghi.
E Phaedro il vecchio: Pace ai detti amari!
ella, buona, cambiava oro con rame.
E stettero, ebbri di vin dolce, un poco
lì nel silenzio opaco della strada.
E la lucerna lor blandia sul capo,
tremula, il serto marcido di rose,
e forse tratta da quel morto olezzo
ronzava un'invisibile falena.
Ma poi la face alla lucerna tutti,
l'un dopo l'altro, accesero. Poi voci
alte destò l'auletride col flauto
doppio, di busso, e tra faville il coro
con un sonoro trepestìo si mosse.

And then there came a lively chorus
of young people through the street at dusk,
their torches extingushed, leaving
a banquet. And Moschus lit his torch from that
lonely lamp, drew near and read in the column:
MYRRHINE SLEEPS BY THE LIGHT OF HER LAMP.
NOW FOR THE FIRST TIME AND FOREVER.
And he said, "Friends, good luck to all of us!
Myrrhine sleeps through the night all alone!
I prayed to the god of Love to finally let
my love for Myrrhine sleep in my heart, at last:
I prayed hard to Love, but the god of Death
heard my prayers." And Callia said: "She was
a bee, and exuded honey, but she pricked
with a stinger." And Agathia said: "In the woods
of love, she mixed thorns, with sweet figs and
mushrooms." But old Phaedro said: "She was kind.
No more bitter words! She gave gold for bronze."
And so they went on for a while, in the dark silent
road, drunk on sweet wine as the light caressed
their heads. And the light trembled, shaking
the rotting garland of roses above their heads:
an invisible moth buzzed around them,
attracted perhaps by the odor of death. But then,
one after another, they all lit their torches
at the lamp. Then, roused by the playing of the double
flute, they raised their voices and, with shuffling
of feet, the chorus stirred onward among the sparks.

L'anima, no. Rimase ancora, e vide
le luci e il canto dileguar lontano.
Era sfuggita al demone che insegna
le vie muffite all'anime dei morti;
gli era sfuggita: or non sapea, da sola,
trovar la strada: e stette ancora ai piedi
del suo sepolcro, al lume vacillante
della sua conscia lampada. E la notte
era al suo colmo, piena d'auree stelle;
quando sentì venire un passo, un pianto
venire acuto, e riconobbe Evèno.
Ché avea perduto il dolce sonno Evèno
da molti giorni, ed or sapea che chiuso
era nell'arca, con la morta etèra.
E singultendo disserrò la porta
del bel tempietto, e presa la lucerna,
entrò. Poi destro, con l'acuta spada,
tentò dell'arca il solido coperchio
e lo mosse, e con ambedue le mani,
puntellando i ginocchi, l'alzò. C'era
con lui, non vista, alle sue spalle, e il lieve
stridìo vaniva nell'anelito aspro
d'Evèno, un'ombra che volea vedere
Myrrhine morta. E questa apparve; e quegli
lasciò d'un urlo ripiombare il marmo
sopra il suo sonno e l'amor suo, per sempre.

Not the spirit, for it stayed behind, and it saw
the lights and the song trail off in the distance.
It was hurrying to get to the daemon who instructs
the spirits of the dead in a life of decaying;
it hurried: but it didn't know, by itself,
how to find the street: and it continued to
stand at the foot of its grave, in the flickering
light of its sentient lamp. And the night was
at its zenith, full of golden stars; when it
heard a footstep coming, a sound of weeping
becoming shriller, and recognized Evanus.
Because he had lost his sweet sleep for many
days, Evanus now knew it was shut up in
the sepulchre with the dead courtesan. And
sobbing, he opened the door of the fine
temple, and seizing the lantern, entered.
Then, with sharp sword in one hand,
he tried to lift the solid cover and moved
it a little, and, using both hands and his knees
to brace himself, he succeeded in raising it.
There it was, the unseen spirit, its wings at
his shoulders, and a low scream escaped from
the gasping Evanus, at this phantom which wanted
to see Myrrhine dead. The body appeared; and he
let out a shriek that caused the marble cover to
fall back over his sleep, on his love, forever.

E fuggì, fuggì via l'anima, e un gallo
rosso cantò con l'aspro inno la vita:
la vita; ed ella si trovò tra i morti.
Né una a tutti era la via di morte,
ma tante e tante, e si perdean raggiando
nell'infinita opacità del vuoto.

Ed era ignota a lei la sua. Ma molte
ombre nell'ombra ella vedea passare
e dileguare: alcune col lor mite
demone andare per la via serene,
ed altre, in vano, ricusar la mano
del lor destino. Ma sfuggita ell'era
da tanti giorni al demone; ed ignota
l'era la via. Dunque si volse ad una
anima dolce e vergine, che andando
si rivolgeva al dolce mondo ancora;
e chiese a quella la sua via. Ma quella,
l'anima pura, ecco che tremò tutta
come l'ombra di un nuovo esile pioppo:
"Non la so!" disse, e nel pallor del Tutto
vanì. L'etèra si rivolse ad una
anima santa e flebile, seduta
con tra le mani il dolce viso in pianto.
Era una madre che pensava ancora
ai dolci figli; ed anche lei rispose:
"Non la so!"; quindi nel dolor del Tutto
sparì. L'etèra errò tra i morti a lungo

And the spirit fled, fled far away, as a red
rooster crowed a harsh hymn to life: to life
but now she sang among the dead:
One of these roads was the way to death,
and little by little, it wandered losing
its light in the infinite darkness of Emptiness.

It didn't know what path to take, then.
But it saw many shadows passing and
vanishing: some with gentle daemon guides
going on their peaceful way, and others,
in vain, refusing the hand of destiny.
But Myrrhine's spirit had come many days
ahead of its guide and it didn't know the way
before its time. So it turned to a sweet virgin
spirit, coming into the gentle world again;
and asked which way the spirit was going. But
that way, that of pure spirit, makes us tremble
in the shade of the slender poplar: "I don't
know!" cried the spirit and vanished
into the light of Everything. The courtesan
turned toward a saintly, mournful spirit
sitting and weeping, and holding its sweet
face in its hands. It was a mother who kept
thinking of her small infants; and again
she responded; "I don't know!" fleeing
into the sadness of Everything. The courtesan
wandered miserably among the dead as

miseramente come già tra i vivi;
ma ora in vano; e molto era il ribrezzo
di là, per l'inquïeta anima nuda
che in faccia a tutti sorgea su nei trivi.

E alfine insonne l'anima d'Evèno
passò veloce, che correva al fiume
arsa di sete, dell'oblìo. Né l'una
l'altra conobbe. Non l'avea mai vista.
Myrrhine corse su dal trivio, e chiese,
a quell'incognita anima veloce,
la strada. Evèno le rispose: "Ho fretta."

E più veloce l'anima d'Evèno
corse, in orrore, e la seguì la trista
anima ignuda. Ma la prima sparve
in lontananza, nella eterna nebbia;
e l'altra, amante, a un nuovo trivio incerto
sostò, l'etèra. E intese là bisbigli,
ma così tenui, come di pulcini
gementi nella cavità dell'uovo.
Era un bisbiglio, quale già l'etèra
s'era ascoltata, con orror, dal fianco
venir su pio, sommessamente... quando
avea, di là, quel suo bel fior di carne,
senza una piega i petali. Ma ora
trasse al sussurro, Myrrhine l'etèra.
Cauta pestava l'erbe alte del prato

it had among the living; but now it was
in vain; and in horror, for the naked
and terrified soul would raise its face
to question everyone at the crossroad.

And at last, sleepless, the spirit of Evanus,
burning with thirst, passed swiftly by, running
toward the River of Forgetting. Neither spirit
knew the other, for they had never seen each other
as spirits. Myrrhine ran to the crossroads
to question this unkown spirit who'd arrived
so swiftly. Evanus answered: "I'm in a hurry."

And the spirit of Evanus ran faster,
in horror, while her sad and naked spirit
followed. But he disappeared into the distance,
into the eternal fog; and the courtesan
stopped at another strange, uncertain
crossroad. And here she heard whisperings,
so slight, that seemed to come from two
chicks still inside the egg. It was a whisper
she'd heard before, in horror, from her own
womb, when in her past life, her body was
a perfect flower, not one petal wrinkled.
But now, Myhrrine, the courtesan,
came closer to the strange whispering.
Her naked spirit cautiously trampled
the high meadow grass and saw,

l'anima ignuda, e riguardava in terra,
tra gl'infecondi caprifichi, e vide.
Vide lì, tra gli asfòdeli e i narcissi,
starsene, informi tra la vita e il nulla,
ombre ancor più dell'ombra esili, i figli
suoi, che non volle. E nelle mani esangui
aveano i fiori delle ree cicute,
avean dell'empia segala le spighe,
per lor trastullo. E tra la morte ancora
erano e il nulla, presso il limitare.
E venne a loro Myrrhine; e gl'infanti
lattei, rugosi, lei vedendo, un grido
diedero, smorto e gracile, e gettando
i tristi fiori, corsero coi guizzi,
via, delle gambe e delle lunghe braccia,
pendule e flosce; come nella strada
molle di pioggia, al risonar d'un passo,
fuggono ranchi ranchi i piccolini
di qualche bodda: tali i figli morti
avanti ancor di nascere, i cacciati
prima d'uscire a domandar pietà!

Ma la soglia di bronzo era lì presso,
della gran casa. E l'atrio ululò tetro
per le vigili cagne di sotterra.
Pur vi guizzò, la turba infante, dentro,
rabbrividendo, e dietro lor la madre
nell'infinita oscurità s'immerse.

among barren wild figs, among
asphodels, among the narcisses,
shapeless things between life and
bitter nothingness, ghostlier still than
the shades of exiles, her own unwanted
infants she had refused, shadows more
than shades, so shapeless. And in their
bloodless hands they held, as playthings,
flowers of hemlock and ears of rye
used to halt their birth. And the threshold
between death and nothingness loomed
close again. And Myhrrine came toward
them; and the wrinkled, milky infants,
seeing her, gave a feeble shriek and threw
away their sad flowers, darting off,
their arms and legs dangling; like little toads
scuttling away to escape when they hear
footsteps echo in the rain-damp streets:
so many infants dead that way before
they were even born, banished
before they could emerge to beg for mercy.

But the bronze threshold of Hades' great house
was near. And the watchdogs of the underworld
howled in the dim entrance hall. The infant
chorus still darted back and forth, inside,
shivering, and in front of them their mother
sank deep into the infinite darkness.

SOLON

Triste il convito senza canto, come
tempio senza votivo oro di doni;
ché questo è bello: attendere al cantore
che nella voce ha l'eco dell'Ignoto.
Oh! nulla, io dico, è bello più, che udire
un buon cantore, placidi, seduti
l'un presso l'altro, avanti mense piene
di pani biondi e di fumanti carni,
mentre il fanciullo dal cratere attinge
vino, e lo porta e versa nelle coppe;
e dire in tanto grazïosi detti,
mentre la cetra inalza il suo sacro inno;
o dell'auleta querulo, che piange,
godere, poi che ti si muta in cuore
il suo dolore in tua felicità.

- Solon, dicesti un giorno tu: Beato
chi ama, chi cavalli ha solidunghi,
cani da preda, un ospite lontano.
Ora te né lontano ospite giova
né, già vecchio, i bei cani né cavalli
di solid'unghia, né l'amore, o savio.
Te la coppa ora giova: ora tu lodi
più vecchio il vino e più novello il canto.
E novelle al Pireo, con la bonaccia
prima e co' primi stormi, due canzoni
oltremarine giunsero. Le reca
una donna d'Eresso. - Apri: rispose;

SOLON

A banquet without song is as sad
as a temple without its golden offerings;
this is what is beautiful: to wait for
a singer who has in her voice an echo
of the Unknown. Oh! Nothing, I say, is
more beautiful than to hear a pleasing voice,
friends seated next to each other before
a table full of loaves of bread and smoking meat
while a young boy pours wine from a bowl
into our cups, nothing more pleasing
than to speak some happy words while
the lyre raises its sacred hymns, and
to enjoy the sorrowful notes of the flute,
while, in your heart, which has been so moved,
its sadness has become your happiness.

"One day, Solon," you said: "Blessed are those
who are in love, who have horses with steady
hooves and friends when far from home."
Now a distant host is of no use to you,
not the finest dogs, nor the steadiest horses,
nor even love, o wise one. Now only
the cup of wine is enjoyable; now you
praise old wine more than a new song.
With news from Piraeus, with calm,
prosperous winds and the first flocks
of birds, two new songs arrived from overseas.
And a woman from Erress arrived. 'Open,'

alla rondine, o Phoco, apri la porta. -
Erano le Anthesterïe: s'apriva
il fumeo doglio e si saggiava il vino.

Entrò, col lume della primavera
e con l'alito salso dell'Egeo,
la cantatrice. Ella sapea due canti:
l'uno, d'amore, l'altro era di morte.
Entrò pensosa; e Phoco le porgeva
uno sgabello d'auree borchie ornato
ed una coppa. Ella sedé, reggendo
la risonante pèctide; ne strinse
tacita intorno ai còllabi le corde;
tentò le corde fremebonde, e disse:

Splende al plenilunïo l'orto; il melo
trema appena d'un tremolio d'argento . . .
Nei lontani monti color di cielo
        sibila il vento.

Mugghia il vento, strepita tra le forre,
su le quercie gettasi... Il mio non sembra
che un tremore, ma è l'amore, e corre,
        spossa le membra!

M'è lontano dalle ricciute chiome,
quanto il sole; sì, ma mi giunge al cuore,
come il sole: bello, ma bello come
        sole che muore.

he replies, 'O Phocus, open the door for the swallow.'
These will be the Anthesterieas: he opened
a smoky vessel and sampled the wine."

She entered with the spring light, this singer,
and with the salt breath of the Aegean.
She knew two songs:
one about love, the other about death.
She entered, thoughtful; and Phocus
offered her a stool decorated in gold,
and a goblet. She sat holding a delicate
and resonant lyre; silently, she turned
the pegs to tune the strings, then plucked
the tremulous strings and sang:

The full moon quivers in Eden; the apple
tree barely quivers in its silver light . . .
in the distant mountains the wind whistles
          through the sky's shades of night.

The wind bellows, tearing through ravines, ripping
up oak trees. Still, it's not myself that seems
to tremble at that now, but Love, growing,
          that weakens my limbs.

But He is as far away from my hair as
the sun, yet he pierces my heart till it dies,
as the sun does: beautiful, but beautiful as
          the sun that dies.

Dileguare! e altro non voglio: voglio
farmi chiarità che da lui si effonda.
Scoglio estremo della gran luce, scoglio
        su la grande onda,

dolce è da te scendere dove è pace:
scende il sole nell'infinito mare;
trema e scende la chiarità seguace
        crepuscolare.

La Morte è questa! il vecchio esclamò. Questo,
ella rispose, è, ospite, l'Amore.
Tentò le corde fremebonde, e disse:

Togli il pianto. È colpa! Sei del poeta
nella casa, tu. Chi dirà che fui?
Piangi il morto atleta: beltà d'atleta
        muore con lui.

Muore la virtù dell'eroe che il cocchio
spinge urlando tra le nemiche schiere;
muore il seno, sì, di Rhodòpi, l'occhio
        del timoniere;

ma non muore il canto che tra il tintinno
della pèctide apre il candor dell'ale.
E il poeta fin che non muoia l'inno,
        vive, immortale,

To fade away, that's all I want: I want
to become the corona that streams from him
or, a far rock, when the sun's last rays, distant,
    rest over the ocean,

For sweet is the descent toward peace:
the sun descends into the infinite ocean;
the glow continues in twilight's wide space
    as the sun descends.

"This is death," the old man cried out, "This,
she answered, "is, on the contrary, Love"
then plucked the quivering strings and sang:

Forget your tears. They're not worthy. You reside
in the poet's realm. Who can say I am done?
Have tears for a dead athlete; after he has died
    his beauty is gone.

The valor of the hero dies, he who, shouting,
drives his chariot in the middle of the enemy,
Rhodopi's breast will end up withering
    like a pilot's eyes,

But not the song that from this tremulous
lyre soars on clear bright wings.
And the poet, for his hymns still please us,
    immortal, still sings,

poi che l'inno (diano le rosee dita
pace al peplo, a noi non s'addice il lutto)
è la nostra forza e beltà, la vita,
    l'anima, tutto!

E chi voglia me rivedere, tocchi
queste corde, canti un mio canto: in quella,
tutta rose rimireranno gli occhi
    Saffo la bella.

Questo era il canto della Morte; e il vecchio
Solon qui disse: Ch'io l'impari, e muoia.

for the hymn (let the fingers leave
peace in the heart, not any unwanted mourning)
is our strength, our beauty, our life
        soul, everything!

And whoever wants to resume again, pluck
these strings, sing one of my songs; he will,
in this, gaze upon a rose that is plucked,
        Sappho, the beautiful.

This was the song of Death. And the old
Solon said: "I want to learn it, and die."

Il sonno di Odisseo

I.

Per nove giorni, e notte e dì, la nave
nera filò, ché la portava il vento
e il timoniere, e ne reggeva accorta
la grande mano d'Odisseo le scotte;
né, lasso, ad altri le cedea, ché verso
la cara patria lo portava il vento.
Per nove giorni, e notte e dì, la nera
nave filò, né l'occhio mai distolse
l'eroe, cercando l'isola rupestre
tra il cilestrino tremolìo del mare;
pago se prima di morir vedesse
balzarne in aria i vortici del fumo.
Nel decimo, là dove era vanito
il nono sole in un barbaglio d'oro,
ora gli apparse non sapea che nero:
nuvola o terra? E gli balenò vinto
dall'alba dolce il grave occhio: e lontano
s'immerse il cuore d'Odisseo nel sonno.

II.

E venne incontro al volo della nave,
ecco, una terra, e veleggiava azzurra
tra il cilestrino tremolìo del mare;
e con un monte ella prendea del cielo,
e giù dal monte spumeggiando i botri

THE SLEEP OF ODYSSEUS

I.

For nine days, night and day, the black
ship flew on, carried by the wind
and the helmsman, and shrewd Odysseus
did not let his great hand leave the tiller;
tired, he trusted no one else, while the wind
carried him toward his beloved country.
For nine days, night and day, the black
ship flew on; never did the eyes of the hero
drift in his search for his rocky island
on the sky blue waves of the sea;
he would be happy if before his death he saw
smoke from his roofs spiraling into the air.
On the tenth day, when the ninth sun
sank into a dazzling sky of gold,
he saw a dark spot but couldn't decipher it.
Was it a cloud or land? Then the flash of the sweet
dawn conquered his heavy eyes: and far
from home the heart of Odysseus fell into sleep.

II.

And the ship, in its flight, encountered
an azure island that seemed to fly at them
on the sky blue waves of the sea;
and then a mountain hid the sky,
and from the mountain ravines of white water

scendean tra i ciuffi dell'irsute stipe;
e ne' suoi poggi apparvero i filari
lunghi di viti, ed a' suoi piedi i campi
vellosi della nuova erba del grano:
e tutta apparve un'isola rupestre,
dura, non buona a pascere polledri,
ma sì di capre e sì di buoi nutrice:
e qua e là sopra gli aerei picchi
morian nel chiaro dell'aurora i fuochi
de' mandrïani; e qua e là sbalzava
il mattutino vortice del fumo,
d'Itaca, alfine: ma non già lo vide
notando il cuore d'Odisseo nel sonno.

III.

Ed ecco a prua dell'incavata nave
volar parole, simili ad uccelli,
con fuggevoli sibili. La nave
radeva allora il picco alto del Corvo
e il ben cerchiato fonte; e se n'udiva
un grufolare fragile di verri;
ed ampio un chiuso si scorgea, di grandi
massi ricinto ed assiepato intorno
di salvatico pero e di prunalbo;
ed il divino mandrïan dei verri,
presso la spiaggia, della nera scorza
spogliava con l'aguzza ascia un querciolo,

flowed through brambles of brushwood;
and on the sides of its hills the long rows
of vines, and at the foot were fields
filled with velvety new stalks of wheat;
and the whole rocky island appeared then,
hard, not good to pasture horses,
but good enough for goats and for oxen:
and then, on the airy summits,
the herdsmen's lights went out in the light
of dawn: the morning smoke from the roofs
spiraled into the air, Ithaca, at last:
but the hero didn't see anything because
the heart of Odysseus was still swimming in sleep.

III.

And now from the bow of the black ship
his words flew, as birds sometimes fly,
with a hissing sound. The ship then skimmed
around the high top of Raven Mountain,
and its fountain rimmed of walls; and one could
hear some boars rooting in the delicate plants;
and see the large flock enclosed by huge stones
and the wall itself crowded on all sides
by wild pear trees and by thorn bushes;
and a god-like herdsman of boars,
at the shore's edge, stripped the black bark
of an oak tree bare with his sharp axe,

e grandi pali a rinforzare il chiuso
poi ne tagliò coi morsi aspri dell'ascia;
e sì e no tra lo sciacquìo dell'onde
giungeva al mare il roco ansar dei colpi,
d'Eumeo fedele: ma non già li udiva
tuffato il cuore d'Odisseo nel sonno.

IV.

E già da prua, sopra la nave, a poppa,
simili a freccie, andavano parole
con fuggevoli fremiti. La nave
era di faccia al porto di Forkyne;
e in capo ad esso si vedea l'olivo,
grande, fronzuto, e presso quello un antro:
l'antro d'affaccendate api sonoro,
quando in crateri ed anfore di pietra
filano la soave opra del miele:
e si scorgeva la sassosa strada
della città: si distinguea, tra il verde
d'acquosi ontani, la fontana bianca
e l'ara bianca, ed una eccelsa casa:
l'eccelsa casa d'Odisseo: già forse
stridea la spola fra la trama, e sotto
le stanche dita ricrescea la tela,
ampia, immortale... Oh! non udì né vide
perduto il cuore d'Odisseo nel sonno.

and cut, from the trunk of an oak, great
posts to strengthen the enclosure;
now and again, amidst the lapping of waves,
those harsh cutting strokes fell from the axe
of faithful Eumaeus: but, not hearing the sound,
the heart of Odysseus dove deep into sleep.

IV.

And soon, from the bow of the ship to the stern, words
flew above the ship like arrows, trembling
and fleeting. The ship was facing
the port of Phorys; and at the head of the harbor
one could see, near the mouth of a cavern,
a huge olive tree facing them: the cavern
was swarming with the sounds of bees,
as when they layer their sweet honey
in hollows and in amphorae of rock:
and if one ran along the pebbled road
from the city; one might make out, among
the green of watery alders, the white fountain
and the white altar, and the queen's house;
Odysseus' Queen's house: already perhaps
the shuttle squeaked against the weft, and
the queen once again wore the ample, immortal
cloth . . . O, but Odysseus heard and saw nothing,
for the heart of Odysseus was woven in sleep.

V.

E su la nave, nell'entrare il porto,
il peggio vinse: sciolsero i compagni
gli otri, e la furia ne fischiò dei venti:
la vela si svoltò, si sbatté, come
peplo, cui donna abbandonò disteso
ad inasprire sopra aereo picco:
ecco, e la nave lontanò dal porto;
e un giovinetto stava già nel porto,
poggiato all'asta dalla bronzea punta:
e il giovinetto sotto il glauco olivo
stava pensoso; ed un veloce cane
correva intorno a lui scodinzolando:
e il cane dalle volte irrequïete
sostò, con gli occhi all'infinito mare;
e com'ebbe le salse orme fiutate,
ululò dietro la fuggente nave:
Argo, il suo cane: ma non già l'udiva
tuffato il cuore d'Odisseo nel sonno.

VI.

E la nave radeva ora una punta
d'Itaca scabra. E tra due poggi un campo
era, ben culto; il campo di Laerte;
del vecchio re; col fertile pometo;
coi peri e meli che Laerte aveva

V.

And on the ship, at the entrance to the port,
the worst happened: the sailors untied
the bags of wind, and the winds raged furiously:
the sail turned, flipped about, like a tunic
that some woman abandoned to dry,
there, on some airy mountain top:
and so the ship sailed far from its port:
but a young man was waiting there in the port,
leaning against his bronze spear, and the boy,
Telemachus, stood pensive under the green
olive tree; and a swift dog wagged
its tail in excitement as it ran around him:
the dog who was running around stopped
with his eyes fixed on the infinite sea;
and after smelling the salty trail of the ship,
the dog howled loudly after it;
Argos, Odysseus' dog; but he never heard it
for the heart of Odysseus had dived deep into sleep.

VI.

And the ship was now racing past a mountain
top on Rocky Ithaca. Between two small hills was
a field, very sacred: the field of Laertes,
the old king, with its fertile orchard;
with its pear and apple trees that Laertes

donati al figlio tuttavia fanciullo;
ché lo seguiva per la vigna, e questo
chiedeva degli snelli alberi e quello:
tredici peri e dieci meli in fila
stavano, bianchi della lor fiorita:
all'ombra d'uno, all'ombra del più bianco,
era un vecchio, poggiato su la marra:
il vecchio, volto all'infinito mare
dove mugghiava il subito tumulto,
limando ai faticati occhi la luce,
riguardò dietro la fuggente nave:
era suo padre: ma non già lo vide
notando il cuore d'Odisseo nel sonno.

VII.

Ed i venti portarono la nave
nera più lungi. E subito aprì gli occhi
l'eroe, rapidi aprì gli occhi a vedere
sbalzar dalla sognata Itaca il fumo;
e scoprir forse il fido Eumeo nel chiuso
ben cinto, e forse il padre suo nel campo
ben culto: il padre che sopra la marra
appoggiato guardasse la sua nave;
e forse il figlio che poggiato all'asta
la sua nave guardasse: e lo seguiva,
certo, e intorno correa scodinzolando
Argo, il suo cane; e forse la sua casa,

had given to his son who was then still a child;
who followed him through the vineyard, and asked
him this and that about the slender trees:
thirteen pear trees and three apple stood
in a row, white with their flowery blossoms:
in the shade of one, in the shade of the whitest one,
was an old man, leaning on his hoe:
the old man, facing the infinite sea
where the storm suddenly roared,
shielded his eyes from the lightning,
and saw the racing ship fly straight away:
it was Odysseus' father; but the hero never saw him,
for the heart of Odysseus was swimming in sleep.

VII.

And the winds carried the black ship
further on. And suddenly the hero opened
his eyes, opened them quickly to see
smoke spiral up from the Ithaca he dreamt of;
and maybe he knew the faithful Eumaeus
in that walled orchard; maybe his father
in the sacred field: his father leaning on a hoe
watching the racing ship fly straight away;
and maybe his son leaning on his spear
watching the ship; and with his son, surely,
wagging his tail and running around him,
Argos, his dog; and maybe his house,

la dolce casa ove la fida moglie
già percorreva il garrulo telaio:
guardò: ma vide non sapea che nero
fuggire per il violaceo mare,
nuvola o terra? e dileguar lontano,
emerso il cuore d'Odisseo dal sonno.

the sweet home where his faithful wife
was now running the garrulous loom:
he looked: he saw but couldn't know for sure
the black fleeting spot on the purple sea,
cloud or land? And it vanished into distance,
as the heart of Odysseus rose from sleep.

III

THE LAST VOYAGE

L' Ultimo Viaggio

I. La pala

Ed il timone al focolar sospese
in Itaca l'Eroe navigatore.
Stanco giungeva da un error terreno,
grave ai garretti, ch'egli avea compiuto
reggendo sopra il grande omero un remo.
Quelli cercava che non sanno il mare
né navi nere dalle rosse prore,
e non miste di sale hanno vivande.
E già più lune s'erano consunte
tra scabre rupi, nel cercare in vano
l'azzurro mare in cui tuffar la luce;
né da gran tempo più sentiva il cielo
l'odor di sale, ma l'odor di verde:
quando gli occorse un altro passeggero,
che disse; e il vento che ululò notturno,
si dibatteva, intorno loro, ai monti,
come orso in una fossa alta caduto:
Uomo straniero, al re tu muovi? Oh! tardo!
Al re, già mondo è nel granaio il grano.
Un dio mandò quest'alito, che soffia
anc'oggi, e ieri ventilò la lolla.
Oggi, o tarda opra, vana è la tua pala.
Disse; ma il cuore tutto rise accorto
all'Eroe che pensava le parole
del morto, cieco, dallo scettro d'oro.
Ché cieco ei vede, e tutto sa pur morto:
tra gli alti pioppi e i salici infecondi,
nella caligo, egli, bevuto al botro

I. The Flail

And the navigator hero had hung his rudder
in Ithaca, his longed-for home.
    He had retraced his path having lost his way,
exhausted and foot-weary, this Odysseus,
carrying on his strong shoulder an oar.
Those he searched for didn't know the sea,
nor recognize the black ships with red prows,
but ate their food without salt from the sea.
And already many moons had burned out
among the rugged cliffs, in the vain search
for the deep blue sea into which their light plunged;
when he sniffed the sky for the smell of salt,
there was only the scent of vegetation.
A man he met on his travels spoke to him;
the wind howled all night and
struggled around them toward the hills,
like a bear fallen into a deep pit.
    "Stranger, are you going to see the king?
Oh! Too late! The king's grain is already
winnowed in his granary. Some god sent this light breeze
that blew yesterday, and even today, funneling
the chaff. Today, oh tardy worker, your flail is useless."
    He said this, but the full heart of Odysseus laughed
warily for he remembered the words
of the prophet Tiresias, with his golden scepter:
he sees everything, and also knows the dead:
among the tall poplars and the barren willows,
in the midst of barren lands, the prophet drank blood

il sangue, disse: Misero, avrai pace
quando il ben fatto remo della nave
ti sia chiamato un distruttor di paglie.
Ed ora il cuore, a quel pensier, gli rise
E disse: Uomo terrestre, ala! non pala!
Ma sia. Ben ora qui fermarla io voglio
nella compatta aridità del suolo.
Un fine ha tutto. In ira a un dio da tempo
io volo foglia a cui s'adira il vento.
E l'altro ancora ad Odisseo parlava:
Chi, donde sei degli uomini? venuto
come, tra noi? Non già per l'aere brullo,
come alcuno dei cigni longicolli,
ma scambiando tra loro i due ginocchi.
Parlami, e narra senza giri il vero.

from ditch water, and said to the hero: "Miserable one,
you will have peace when your well-made
ship's oar is taken for a flail by some peasants."
And so the full heart of the hero smiled at this thought:
     He said "Man of the soil, it's an oar! Not a flail!
But so be it. I'll plant this oar in this arid,
Hard soil. Everyone comes to an end.
A god gave this weather in anger where I was
Tossed about like a leaf on the angry winds."
     And the other again spoke to Odysseus:
"Who are your men and where are they from?
How have you come to us? Not from thin air
like one of the long necked swans,
but from between two knees.
Tell me straight and do not twist the truth."

II. L'ALA

E rispose l'Eroe molto vissuto:
Tutto ti narro senza giri il vero.
Sono, a voi sconosciuti, uomini, anch'essi
mortali sì, ma, come dei, celesti,
che non coi piedi, come i lenti bovi,
vanno, e con la vicenda dei ginocchi,
ma con la spinta delle aeree braccia,
come gli uccelli, ed hanno il color d'aria
sotto sé, vasto. Io vidi viaggiando
sbocciar le stelle fuor del cielo infranto,
sotto questi occhi, e il guidator del Carro
venir con me fischiando ai buoi lontano,
e l'auree rote lievi sbalzar sulla
tremola ghiaia della strada azzurra.
Né sempre l'ali noi tra cielo e cielo
battiamo: spesso noi prendiamo il vento:
a mezzo un ringhio acuto, per le froge
larghe prendiamo il vano vento folle,
che ci conduca, e con la forte mano
le briglie io reggo per frenarlo al passo.
Ma un dio ce n'odia, come voi la terra
odia, che voi sostenta sì, ma spezza.
Ch'ha tutto un fine. Or tu fa che un torello
dal re mi venga, ed un agnello e un verro;
che qui ne onori quell'ignoto iddio.
E l'altro ancora rispondea stupito:
L'ignoto è grande, e grande più, se dio.
Or vieni al re, che raddolcito ha il cuore

II. The Wing

And the well-traveled hero answered:
"All I tell you is the truth, without any twists.
I am already known to you men, but there are
men, mortal, yes, but like gods from heaven,
who do not move on their feet like the slow oxen,
shifting from one knee to another,
but work their oars like the wings of birds,
birds that have the vast blue of the sea
under them. On my journeys I have seen,
with these very eyes, stars blossoming in a broken
sky, with my guiding constellation, Ursa Major,
while the driver whistles in the dark distance,
and light, golden wheels bob gently up
the flickering gravel of our blue road.
Our wings do not always carry us between one
sky and the other: often a giant wind takes us:
in the air, there's a loud snarl from huge
nostrils and a crazy wind grabs us
and drives us, but with my powerful hand
I hold the reins and control our pace.
The sea god does not hate us, as the land hates
you, though you continue, broken, but hopeful.
But everything comes to an end: Now I sacrifice
to the king, a small bull, a lamb, and a boar;
though there they honor only an unknown god."
    And the other man, the listener, answers, surprised:
"The unknown is a great and even greater god.
Come now to a king who has a soft heart

oggi, che il grano gli avanzò le corbe.
Così l'eroe divino in una forra
selvosa il remo suo piantò, la lieve
ala incrostata dalla salsa gromma.
Al dio sdegnato per il suo Ciclope,
egli uccise un torello ed un agnello
e terzo un verro montator di scrofe;
e poi discese, e insieme a lui più lune
vennero, e l'una dopo l'altra ognuna
sé, girando tra roccie aspre, consunse.
L'ultima, piena tremolò sul mare
riscintillante, e su la bianca sabbia,
piccola e nera gli mostrò la nave,
e i suoi compagni, ch'attendean guardando
a monte, muti. Ed ei salpò. Sbalzare
vide ancora le rote auree del Carro
sopra le ghiaie dell'azzurra strada:
rivide il fumo salir su, rivide
Itaca scabra, e la sua grande casa.
Dove il timone al focolar sospese.

today and whose grain fills the bushels."
    So the divine hero plants his oar, that light wing,
encrusted with sea salt, in a woody ravine.
To the god despised by the Cyclops, he offers
these three: a lamb and a boar mounting a sow;
and afterwards he went down and many moons
crossed the sky, one after the other, rotating over
the rough cliffs, until each of them burnt out.
Finally, when the sparkling sea is above high tide,
surrounding the black ship on the white sand, and
the prodigy and his companions, who were
waiting and watching from the mountains, are
thoughtful, they set sail. The hero sees the golden wheel
of the chariot toss up gravel on his blue path again:
again he sees the salt spray, sees rugged Ithaca
and his own spacious longed-for home.
    And there he would hang the rudder by the hearth.

III. Le gru nocchiere

E un canto allora venne a lui dall'alto,
di su le nubi, di raminghe gru.
Sospendi al fumo ora il timone, e dormi.
Le Gallinelle fuggono lo strale
già d'Orïone, e son cadute in mare.
Rincalza su la spiaggia ora la nave
nera con pietre, che al ventar non tremi,
Eroe; ché sono per soffiare i venti.
L'alleggio della stiva apri, che l'acqua
scoli e non faccia poi funghir le doghe,
Eroe; ché sono per cader le pioggie.
Sospendi al fumo ora il timone, e in casa
tieni all'asciutto i canapi ritorti,
ogni arma, ogni ala della nave, e dormi.
Ché viene il verno, viene il freddo acuto
che fa nei boschi bubbolar le fiere
che fuggono irte con la coda al ventre:
quando a tre piedi, il filo della schiena
rotto a metà, la grigia testa bassa,
il vecchio va sotto la neve bianca;
e il randagio pitocco entra dal fabbro,
nella fucina aperta, e prende sonno
un poco al caldo tra l'odor di bronzo.
Navigatore di cent'arti, dormi
nell'alta casa, o, se ti piace, solca
ora la terra, dopo arata l'onda.
Questo era canto che rodeva il cuore
del timoniere, che volgea la barra
verso un approdo, e tedio avea dell'acqua;

III. The Pilot Cranes

And just then a song came to him from high,
from the clouds, from the wandering cranes.
    Now, hero, near the smoky fire, hang the rudder, and sleep.
The stars of the Pleiades already flee before
the arrow of Orion and the sun falls into the sea.
Now, hero, prop up the ship with black stones
so that it won't buffet in the wind; the strong
winds are about to blow too harshly.
Hero, unlock the hold and let the water
drain so the cargo won't mold. Stand
the rudder by the smoky fire; store all the ropes
that are dry and rolled up, all the weapons, all the ship's
canvas sails in the wheelhouse, sleep.
When winter comes, the biting cold comes
that makes even wild beasts in forests shiver
and flee with their bristling tails at their stomachs:
someone on three feet, the spine of the back about
to break, and with a gray head lowered,
an old man, staggers in the white snow;
and so this wandering beggar enters the blacksmith's
near the open forge, sleeps a little in the heat
with the smell of metal all around him.
Navigator of a hundred deceitful wiles, sleep
in your house up high, and then, if it pleases you,
plow the earth, until you'll plow the waves.
    This was the song that gnawed at the heart
of the helmsman, who then turned the helm toward
a landing place, weary finally of the water;

ché passavano, agli uomini gridando
giunto il maltempo, venti nevi pioggie,
e lo sparire delle stelle buone;
e tra le nubi esse con fermo cuore,
gittando rauche grida alla burrasca,
andavano, e coi remi battean l'aria.

the cranes pass over, and the bad weather comes
shouting to the men, winds, snow, rains,
and the guiding stars vanish with the storm;
and yet through the clouds, they, with constant heart,
throw these harsh words to the storm, and
they go on, and with their wings, like oars, beat the air.

IV. Le gru guerriere

Dicean, Dormi, al nocchiero, Ara, al villano,
di su le nubi, le raminghe gru.
Ara: la stanga dell'aratro al giogo
lega dei bovi; ché tu n'hai, ben d'erbe
sazi, in capanna, o figlio di Laerte.
Fatti col cuoio d'un di loro, ucciso,
un paio d'uose, che difenda il freddo,
ma prima il dentro addenserai di feltro;
e cucirai coi tendini del bove
pelli de' primi nati dalle capre,
che a te dall'acqua parino le spalle;
e su la testa ti porrai la testa
d'un vecchio lupo, che ti scaldi, e i denti
bianchi digrigni tra il nevischio e i venti.
Arare il campo, non il mare, è tempo,
da che nel cielo non si fa vedere
più quel branchetto delle sette stelle.
Sessanta giorni dopo volto il sole,
quando ritorni il conduttor del Carro,
allor dolce è la brezza, il mare è calmo;
brilla Boote a sera, e sul mattino
tornata già la rondine cinguetta,
che il mare è calmo e che dolce è la brezza.
La brezza chiama a sé la vela, il mare
chiama a sé il remo; e resta qua canoro
il cuculo a parlare al vignaiolo.
Questo era canto che mordeva il cuore
a chi non bovi e sol avea l'aratro;

IV. The Warlike Cranes

The wandering cranes say, "Sleep," to the pilot.
"Plow," they say to the farmer, from the clouds above
each one. *Plow: tie the shaft of the plow to*
the oxen's yoke; they are all well fed on hay
from the barn; look to what you don't have, son of Laertes.
Make, with the hide of a slaughtered ox,
a pair of leggings to protect you from the cold:
but first of all, fill the inside with felt,
then sew together, with tendons from the ox,
skins of first born kids to cover
your shoulders from rain water:
and on your head put the head an old wolf
you hunted, to keep you warm, whose white fangs
will devour the sleet and the winds.
It is time to plow the field, not the sea,
from which you can see not even a handful
of seven stars in the Great Bear. It's sixty days
until the sun returns, until the Great Bear, the stars
that guide you, will return. Then the breeze will be sweet,
the sea calm, the brilliant huntsman will be visible
and in the mornings, you will hear
the chattering of a swallow that has
also returned. Now the sea is calm, the breeze is sweet,
the breeze calls to the sail, the sea
calls to the oar, and even a cuckoo is melodious
and sings to the plowman in the vineyard.
    This was the song that gnawed the heart
of him who had no ox, only a plow—and so

ch'egli ha bel dire, Prestami il tuo paro!
Son le faccende, ed ora ogni bifolco
semina, e poi, sicuro della fame,
ode venti fischiare, acque scrosciare,
ilare. E intanto esse, le gru, moveano
verso l'Oceano, a guerra, in righe lunghe,
empiendo il cielo d'un clangor di trombe.

he spoke these fine words: "Give me two oxen.
Then prepare to till." He makes ready to depart,
every plowman seeds his fields, secure in his reputation,
and hears the wind whistle, the spring rain beat down.
In the meantime, the cranes move toward
the ocean, to the struggle, in straight lines,
filling the sky with the clamor of their trumpets.

V. Il remo confitto

E per nove anni al focolar sedeva,
di sua casa, l'Eroe navigatore:
ché più non gli era alcuno error marino
dal fato ingiunto e alcuno error terrestre.
Sì, la vecchiaia gli ammollia le membra
a poco a poco. Ora dovea la morte
fuori del mare giungergli, soave,
molto soave, e né coi dolci strali
dovea ferirlo, ma fiatar leggiera
sopra la face cui già l'uragano
frustò, ma fece divampar più forte.
E i popoli felici erano intorno,
che il figlio, nato lungi alle battaglie,
savio reggeva in abbondevol pace.
Crescean nel chiuso del fedel porcaio
floridi i verri dalle bianche zanne,
e nei ristretti pascoli più tanti
erano i bovi dalle larghe fronti,
e tante più dal Nerito le capre
pendean strappando irsuti pruni e stipe,
e molto sotto il tetto alto giaceva
oro, bronzo, olezzante olio d'oliva.
Ma raro nella casa era il convito,
né più sonava l'ilare tumulto
per il grande atrio umbratile; ché il vecchio
più non bramava terghi di giovenco,
né coscie gonfie d'adipe, di verro;
amava, invano, la fioril vivanda,

V. The Tethered Oar

And for nine years the heroic seaman
remained seated there by his own fireside:
for there were no more wanderings on the sea
imposed by fate and no more problems on land.
Yes, old age had softened his body
little by little. Now the death that might come
to him there on the sea would be sweet,
very sweet, and not like the soft arrows
that had wounded him, for now he breathed
the air thoughtlessly, he who had been worn
down by the storm, but only burned more
brightly now. And grateful people surround
the son who was born far from battle
and who now rules wisely in a lasting peace.
Eumaeus' pens are full and the boars
with their white tusks thrive there
and are not restricted to confining pastures,
nor are the cattle with their wide foreheads
nor the goats from Mt. Nerito snatching
and tearing at the thorn bushes,
and under the high roof, an abundance
of gold, bronze, and sweet-smelling olive oil.
But banquets were rare in that house
and cheerful shouts no longer resounded
in the large, dim hall; the old man
no longer longed for large roasts
or for the leg of a fattened boar;
he loved in vain the life-giving flower,

il dolce loto, cui chi mangia, è pago,
né altro chiede che brucar del loto.
Così le soglie dell'eccelsa casa
or d'Odissèo dimenticò l'aedo
dai molti canti, e il lacero pitocco,
che l'un corrompe e l'altro orna il convito.
E il Laertiade ora vivea solingo
fuori del mare, come il vecchio remo
scabro di salsa gromma, che piantato
lungi avea dalle salse aure nel suolo,
e strettolo, ala, tra le glebe gravi.
E il grigio capo dell'Eroe tremava,
avanti al mormorare della fiamma,
come là, nella valle solitaria,
quel remo al soffio della tramontana.

the sweet lotus, sweet to eat and satisfying,
and asked to drink nothing but the lotus.
Thus on the steps of the lofty house
of the now forgetful Odysseus stood the poet
of many songs and also the worn-out beggar:
one corrupts, the other decorates the banquet.
And so the son of Laertes now lived alone
without the sea, like an old oar
rough with encrusted salt that had long
been far from the salt of the sea,
but, confined there, oppressed by the land.
And the gray head of the hero trembled
in front of the murmuring flames,
there in the solitary valley,
like an oar blasted by the north wind.

VI. Il fuso al fuoco

E per nove anni ogni anno udì la voce,
di su le nubi, delle gru raminghe
che diceano, Ara, che diceano, Dormi;
ed alternando squilli di battaglia
coi remi in lunghe righe battean l'aria:
mentre noi guerreggiamo, ara, o villano;
dormi, o nocchiero, noi veleggeremo.
E il canto il cuore dell'Eroe mangiava,
chiuso alle genti come un aratore
cui per sementa mancano i due bovi.
Sedeva al fuoco, e la sua vecchia moglie,
la bene oprante, contro lui sedeva,
tacita. E per le fauci del camino
fuligginose, allo spirar de' venti
umidi, ardeano fisse le faville;
ardean, lievi sbraciando, le faville
sul putre dorso dei lebeti neri.
Su quelle intento si perdea con gli occhi
avvezzi al cielo il corridor del mare.
E distingueva nel sereno cielo
le fuggitive Pleiadi e Boote
tardi cadente e l'Orsa, anche nomata
il Carro, che lì sempre si rivolge,
e sola è sempre del nocchier compagna.
E il fulgido Odisseo dava la vela
al vento uguale, e ferree avea le scotte,
e i buoni suoi remigatori stanchi
poneano i remi lungo le scalmiere.

VI. THE SPINDLE BY THE HEARTH

Every year for nine years he heard the voice
of the wandering cranes from high in the clouds:
saying to him, "Plow," saying to him, "Sleep,"
and alternating trumpet blasts of battle
with the oars in a straight line beating their song:
While we make war you are plowing, o farmer;
and you sleep, o pilot, while we are sailing.
And the dream song ate at the heart of the hero,
closed as it was to people like the farmer
who needs two oxen in order to sow seed.
He sat still at his hearth, with his old wife,
that doer of good deeds, who sat across
from him, silent. And through the sooty flue
of the chimney and with its drafty exhalations,
sparks shone brightly, and with the embers
steadily spreading, under the rotting back
of the black, three-legged pot, the hero dreamt.
He had lost his purpose, as one who has eyes
accustomed to the sky and the racing sea.
And he dreamt that in the peaceful sky were
the fugitive Pleiades and Bootes,
slowly falling, and the Bear, also known as
the Cart, that always revolves around itself,
and the Sun, always the pilot's companion.
        And this way the dazzling Odysseus hoisted sail,
and to catch the wind, made the sheets taut
so his good oarsmen, tired of rowing,
could place their long oars on the sides of the ship.

La nave con uno schioccar di tela
correa da sé nella stellata notte,
e prendean sonno i marinai su i banchi,
e lei portava il vento e il timoniere.
L'Eroe giaceva in un'irsuta pelle,
sopra coperta, a poppa della nave,
e, dietro il capo, si fendeva il mare
con lungo scroscio e subiti barbagli.
Egli era fisso in alto, nelle stelle,
ma gli occhi il sonno gli premea, soave,
e non sentiva se non sibilare
la brezza nelle sartie e nelli stragli.
E la moglie appoggiata all'altro muro
faceva assiduo sibilare il fuso.

The ship with one tear in its canvas sail
ran on by itself in the starlit night,
with the sailors falling asleep on its decks,
while the wind and the helmsman guided them.
The hero rested under a shaggy hide
on the upper deck near the stern of the ship
while behind his head, the sea split wide open
with a crack of thunder and a glare of light.
He was intent on the stars and the sky,
but his eyes were closing gently into sleep,
and he did not sense that the breeze was not
whistling in the ropes tying the shaft to the stay.
    And his wife leaned against the opposite wall
and carefully kept the spindle whistling.

VII. La zattera

E gli dicea la veneranda moglie:
Divo Odisseo, mi sembra oggi quel giorno
che ti rividi. Io ti sedea di contro,
qui, nel mio seggio. Stanco eri di mare,
eri, divo Odisseo, sazio di sangue!
Come ora. Muto io ti vedeva al lume
del focolare, fissi gli occhi ingiù.
Fissi in giù gli occhi, presso la colonna,
egli taceva: ché ascoltava il cuore
suo che squittiva come cane in sogno.
E qualche foglia d'ellera sul ciocco
secco crocchiava, e d'uno stizzo il vento
uscìa fischiando; ma l'Eroe crocchiare
udiva un po' la zattera compatta,
opera sua nell'isola deserta.
Su la decimottava alba la zattera
egli sentì brusca salire al vento
stridulo; e l'uomo su la barca solo
era, e sola la barca era sul mare:
soli con qualche errante procellaria.
E di là donde tralucea già l'alba
ora appariva una catena fosca
d'aeree nubi, e torbide a prua l'onde
picchiavano; ecco e si sventò la vela.
E l'uomo allora udì di contro un canto
di torte conche, e divinò che dietro
quelle il nemico, il truce dio del mare,
venìa tornando ai suoi cerulei campi.

VII. The Raft

And the hero's adoring wife said to him:
"Divine Odysseus, I feel this is like the day
I saw you again, sat across from you
here in this seat. You were weary of the sea,
you are, divine Odysseus, tired of blood!
Just now I saw you standing mute in the light
of the fireplace with your eyes so downcast."
He stared down, fixing his eyes to the column,
standing speechless: whatever he heard deep in
his heart yelped like a sleeping dog in its dream.
Some leaves of ivy on a piece of wood
crackled and a peevish wind began to moan,
then whistle; but what the hero heard was the creaking
sound of the solid raft he had built himself,
while stranded on the deserted island.
When he had passed ten dawns on
the raft, he felt a shrill wind rise suddenly;
and the man was alone on the raft
and the raft was alone on the sea:
both of them alone with some wandering birds.
And from where the dawn had just broken through to
daylight, there now appeared a dark chain of clouds
in the sky; muddy waves splashed over the prow.
How they played havoc with the sail of the raft!
And Odysseus heard from across the sea,
the call of the conch shell; he guessed that his enemy
was in the rear, the fierce sea god,
returning to his sky-blue fields. The god saw

Lui vide, e rise il dio con uno schianto
secco di tuono che rimbombò tetro;
e venne. Udiva egli lo sciabordare
delle ruote e il nitrir degli ippocampi.
E volavano al cielo alto le schiume
dalle lor bocche masticanti il morso;
e l'uragano fumido di sghembo
sferzava lor le groppe di serpente.
Soli nel mare erano l'uomo e il nume
e il nume ergeva su l'ondate il torso
largo, e scoteva il gran capo; e tra il nembo
folgoreggiava il lucido tridente.
E il Laertiade al cuore suo parlava,
ch'altri non v'era; e sotto avea la barra.

the man and laughed with a dry crack of thunder,
which resounded as the sea god came close.
The man heard a splashing of chariot wheels
and the neighing of sea horses pulling it.
As they flew to the sky their mouths were foaming,
they chewed at the bit as a twisting hurricane
of smoke arose, whipping their backs with serpents.
The man was alone in the sea with the god
and the god had risen up out of the waves,
torso erect, head on fire; lightning striking,
between the clouds, from his shining trident.
    The son of Laertes spoke from his heart, for
no one else was there, and he had the helm.

VIII. Le rondini

E per nove anni egli aspettò la morte
che fuor del mare gli dovea soave
giungere; e sì, nel decimo, su l'alba,
giunsero a lui le rondini, dal mare.
Egli dormia sul letto traforato
cui sosteneva un ceppo d'oleastro
barbato a terra; e marinai sognava
parlare sparsi per il mare azzurro.
E si destò con nell'orecchio infuso
quel vocìo fioco; ed ascoltò seduto:
erano rondini, e sonava intorno
l'umbratile atrio per il lor sussurro.
E si gittò sugli Omeri le pelli
caprine, ai piedi si legò le dure
uose bovine: e su la testa il lupo
facea nell'ombra biancheggiar le zanne.
E piano uscì dal talamo, non forse
udisse il lieve cigolio la moglie;
ma lei teneva un sonno alto, divino,
molto soave, simile alla morte.
E il timone staccò dal focolare,
affumicato, e prese una bipenne.
Ma non moveva il molto accorto al mare,
subito, sì per colli irti di quercie,
per un vïotterello aspro, e mortali
trovò ben pochi per la via deserta;
e disse a un mandriano segaligno,
che per un pioppo secco era la scure;

VIII. THE SWALLOWS

And for nine years he had waited for
death to come for him gently, away
from the sea; and thus, in the tenth year,
at about dawn, swallows arrived for him
from the sea. He was sleeping
on a bed held by a wild olive rooted
deep in the earth; and he dreamed of the talk
of his sailors scattered across the blue sea.
Then, he was wide awake and a faint sound
filled his ear; and he listened, sitting there,
for the swallows had come and their sound rang
throughout the shady hall, though they whispered.
And so he had thrown goat skins over his shoulders,
to his feet, he had fastened stiff leggings made
from cow skin: and above, the head of a wolf
with fangs that shone white in the shadows.
And quietly he came out of his bedroom,
in case his wife had heard the soft creaking;
but she rested in a sleep that was deep, divine,
very gentle and almost like the sleep of the dead.
　　And so he took the rudder from the smoky fireside
and on his way grabbed hold of a two-edged axe.
　　But that very wily man did not move straight
or directly to the sea, but along a trail full of oaks
and through a rough, narrow and deadly route
he found his way in a short time to the deserted path:
he told a weather-beaten shepherd
that the axe was for a dying poplar tree;

e disse ad una riccioluta ancella,
che per uno stabbiolo era il timone:
così parlava il tessitor d'inganni,
e non senz'ali era la sua parola.
E poi soletto deviò volgendo
l'astuto viso al fresco alito salso.
Le quercie ai piedi gli spargean le foglie
roggie che scricchiolavano al suo passo.
Gemmava il fico, biancheggiava il pruno,
e il pero avea ne' rosei bocci il fiore.
E di su l'alto Nerito il cuculo
contava arguto il su e giù de l'onde.
E già l'Eroe sentiva sotto i piedi
non più le foglie ma scrosciar la sabbia;
né più pruni fioriti, ma vedeva
i giunchi scabri per i bianchi nicchi;
e infine apparve avanti al mare azzurro
l'Eroe vegliardo col timone in collo
e la bipenne; e l'inquieto mare,
mare infinito, fragoroso mare,
su la duna lassù lo riconobbe
col riso innumerevole dell'onde.

and then he told a curly-headed maidservant
to find the rudder behind a small cowshed;
thus spoke the weaver of many deceptions
and his words were not without wings.
And then, alone, the devious one turned
his crafty face toward the cool, briny wind.
The oaks scattered their rusty leaves at his feet
for him over brambles that crunched at his step.
The fig tree was full of fruit, the thorn bush flowered
white, and the pear tree had rosy buds in flower.
And from above, high in the darkness, the cuckoo
counted the waves in the sea. And already
the hero felt under his feet not more leaves
but the crunching of sand; not more ripe figs
but the gnarled rushes and reeds next to seashells;
and finally the old hero stood before the blue sea,
an old man with a rudder and an axe; and there
was the restless sea, the infinite sea,
the crashing sea, and up there on the dune,
he knows again the endless laugh of the waves.

IX. Il pescatore

Ma lui vedendo, ecco di subito una
rondine deviò con uno strillo.
Ch'ella tornava. Ora Odisseo con gli occhi
cercava tutto il grigio lido curvo,
s'egli vedesse la sua nave in secco.
Ma non la vide; e vide un uomo, un vecchio
di triti panni, chino su la sabbia
raspare dove boccheggiava il mare
alternamente. A lui fu sopra, e disse:
Abbiamo nulla, o pescator di rena?
Ben vidi, errando su la nave nera,
uomo seduto in uno scoglio aguzzo
reggere un filo pendulo sul flutto;
ma il lungo filo tratto giù dal piombo
porta ai pesci un adunco amo di bronzo
che sì li uncina; e ne schermisce il morso
un liscio cerchio di bovino corno.
Ché l'uomo, quando è roso dalla fame,
mangia anche il sacro pesce che la carne
cruda divora. Io vidi, anzi, mortali
gittar le reti dalle curve navi,
sempre aliando sui pescosi gorghi,
come le folaghe e gli smerghi ombrosi.
E vidi i pesci nella grigia sabbia
avvoltolarsi, per desìo dell'acqua,
versati fuori della rete a molte
maglie; e morire luccicando al sole.
Ma non vidi senz'amo e senza rete

IX. The Fisherman

But then a swallow, suddenly seeing him,
and with a shriek, swerved to avoid Odysseus.
Then circled around toward where the eyes
of the hero searched the whole gray curve of beach,
hoping to see his ship washed up on shore.
But he did not find it there; instead he saw a man,
stooped, old, in filthy rags, standing on the beach,
alternately scratching at the sand and gasping
into the sea. Standing above him, Odysseus smiled,
    "Caught anything yet, o fisherman of the sands?
I've seen, while wandering in my black ship,
a man seated on a sharp reef,
holding up a line hanging over the waves,
the long line held down by a lead sinker
which carried to the fish a bent hook made of bronze,
which thus hooks them; a loop of cow's horn
keeps them from biting off the bait to escape.
The man, when he was flushed with hunger
ate even the sacred fish which devours
raw flesh! I saw as well, men
throwing nets from curved ships
that hovered over fish-filled whirlpools,
diving like moor hens and cormorants.
And I also saw fish in the gray sand
flop around gasping for water,
spilling out of well-knotted
nets, and soon die, shining in the sun.
But I have not seen, without hook or net,

niuno mai fare tali umide prede,
o vecchio, e niuno farsi mai vivanda
di tali scabre chiocciole dell'acqua,
che indosso hanno la nave, oppur dei granchi,
che indosso hanno l'incudine dei fabbri.
E il malvestito al vecchio Eroe rispose:
Tristo il mendico che al convito sdegna
cibo che lo scettrato re gli getta,
sia tibia ossuta od anche pingue ventre.
Ché il Tutto, buono, ha tristo figlio: il Niente.
Prendo ciò che il mio grande ospite m'offre,
che dona, cupo brontolando in cuore,
ma dona: il mare fulgido e canoro,
ch'è sordo in vero, ma più sordo è l'uomo.
Or al mendico il vecchio Eroe rispose:
O non ha la rupestre Itaca un buono
suo re ch'ha in serbo molto bronzo e oro?
che verri impingua, negli stabbi, e capre?
cui molto odora nei canestri il pane?
Non forse il senno d'Odisseo qui regge,
che molto errò, molto in suo cuor sofferse?
e fu pitocco e malvestito anch'esso.
Non sai la casa dal sublime tetto,
del Laertiade fulgido Odisseo?

anyone take such damp spoils, old man—
and nobody ever finds a meal with no hook
or taking those misshapen snails from the water
which look like they have ships on their backs
or crabs, that seem to have anvils on their backs."
　　And the ragged old man answered the hero,
"Sad is the beggar who scorns food at a banquet
when it is thrown to him by the king,
whether he has bony shins or a fat belly.
The other side of All is Nothing.
I take whatever my great host offers me, even
if he gives it grumbling, with a hollow heart.
The shining melodious sea is deaf in truth,
but even more profoundly deaf is man."
　　Now the old hero replied to the beggar,
"Does not rocky Ithaca have a good king
who has stored bronze and gold in reserve?
Who has fattened boars and goats in the sty?
Who scents the baskets with much bread?
Perhaps this isn't the wisdom of Odysseus, who
governed, who wandered, who suffered in his heart?
And he was a beggar in rags himself.
Don't you know the exalted house
of shining Odysseus, son of Laertes?"

X. La conchiglia

Il malvestito non volgeva il capo
dal mare alterno, ed al ricurvo orecchio
teneva un'aspra tortile conchiglia,
come ascoltasse. Or all'Eroe rispose:
O Laertiade fulgido Odisseo,
so la tua casa. Ma non io pitocco
querulo sono, poi che fui canoro
eroe, maestro io solo a me. Trovai
sparsi nel cuore gl'infiniti canti.
A te cantai, divo Odisseo, da quando
pieno di morti fu l'umbratile atrio,
simili a pesci quali il pescatore
lasciò morire luccicando al sole.
E vedo ancor le schiave moriture
terger con acqua e con porose spugne
il sangue, e molto era il singulto e il grido.
A te cantavo, e tu bevendo il vino
cheto ascoltavi. E poi t'increbbe il detto
minor del fatto. Ascolto or io l'aedo,
solo, in silenzio. Ché gittai la cetra,
io. La raccolse con la mano esperta
solo di scotte un marinaio, un vecchio
dagli occhi rossi. Or chi la tocca? Il vento.
Or all'Aedo il vecchio Eroe rispose:
Terpiade Femio, e me vecchiezza offese
e te: ché tolse ad ambedue piacere
ciò che già piacque. Ma non mai che nuova
non mi paresse la canzon più nuova

X. The Seashell

The beggar did not turn his head
from that other sea, but held to his bent ear
a rough and tortoise-like seashell, as though
he listened. And he responded to the hero:
  "O glorious Odysseus, son of the tribe of Laertes,
I know your house. And no, I am not a beggar
who is complaining, even though back then I sang
heroically songs I taught to myself.
I found endless songs scattered in my heart.
I sang to you, divine Odysseus, when
the dead filled the shadowy entrance hall
in the way fish are left by fishermen
to die, glittering in the sun. And I still
see the enslaved girls doomed to die,
their blood wiped away with water and useless,
porous sponges, so many cries and sobs.
I have sung to you while you were drinking wine
and heard only silence. For you, a word
was less than a deed. I am a listener,
 a poet, alone, in the silence. Because
I have thrown away the lyre. But it was
caught by an old sailor whose hand had practiced
on sails. And the old man had red eyes. But
who has touched the lyre? Only the wind."
And now the old hero replied to the poet:
  "Femius, of the tribe of artists, old age
offends you and me: because old age takes away
both present pleasure and that which formerly
gave pleasure, but not the pleasure of your new songs,

di Femio, o Femio; più nuova e più bella:
m'erano vecchie d'Odisseo le gesta.
Sonno è la vita quando è già vissuta:
sonno; ché ciò che non è tutto, è nulla.
Io, desto alfine nella patria terra,
ero com'uomo che nella novella
alba sognò, né sa qual sogno, e pensa
che molto è dolce a ripensar qual era.
Or io mi voglio rituffar nel sonno,
s'io trovi in fondo dell'oblio quel sogno.
Tu verrai meco. Ma mi narra il vero:
qual canto ascolti, di qual dolce aedo?
Ch'io non so, nella scabra isola, che altri
abbia nel cuore inseminati i canti.
E il vecchio Aedo al vecchio Eroe rispose:
Questo, di questo. Un nicchio vile, un lungo
tortile nicchio, aspro di fuori, azzurro
di dentro, e puro, non, Eroe, più grande
del nostro orecchio; e tutto ha dentro il mare,
con le burrasche e le ritrose calme,
coi venti acuti e il ciangottìo dell'acque.
Una conchiglia, breve, perché l'oda
il breve orecchio, ma che il tutto v'oda;
tale è l'Aedo. Pure a te non piacque.
Con un sorriso il vecchio Eroe rispose:
Terpiade Femio, assai più grande è il mare!

Femius, O Femius: the newer, the more beautiful.
They were to me like the old exploits of Odysseus.
Sleep is life when life has already been lived:
sleep; because what is not everything is nothing.
I, awake at last in my native country,
will be like the man in a novel who dreams,
but at daybreak never knows what his dream is
and senses much that is sweet has been remembered
from another time. I wish to plunge again
into sleep, so that I may find that dream in oblivion.
Come with me. But tell me the truth:
that song you heard, which sweet poet wrote it?
I do not know that even on this rough island
other hearts have been seeded with song."
And the old poet responded to the old hero:
    "This one, or that one. A worthless shell,
a spiral shell, rough on the outside, but blue
on the inside, it has clarity, hero, not bigger
than our ear's; and all have been in the sea
with the storms and the nets, but calm
when winds are sharp and the water billows.
A seashell, a small one, because only a small ear
is listening and hears all it can hear;
such is the poet. Clear, but did not please you."
    With a smile the old hero responded:
"O Femius, you artist, the sea is greater than us!"

XI. LA NAVE IN SECCO

E il vecchio Aedo e il vecchio Eroe movendo
seguian la spiaggia del sonante mare,
molto pensando, e là, sul curvo lido,
piccola e nera, apparve lor la nave.
Vedean la poppa, e n'era lunga l'ombra
sopra la sabbia; né molt'alto il sole.
E sopra lei bianchi tra mare e cielo
galleggiavano striduli gabbiani.
E vide l'occhio dell'Eroe che fresca
era la pece: e vide che le pietre
giaceano in parte, ché placato il vento
già non faceva più brandir la nave;
e vide in giro dagli scalmi acuti
pender gli stroppi di bovino cuoio;
e vide dal righino alto di poppa
sporger le pale di ben fatti remi.
Gli rise il cuore, poi che pronta al corso
era la nave; e le moveva intorno,
come al carro di guerra agile auriga
prima di addurre i due cavalli al giogo.
E venuto alla prua rossa di minio,
sopra la sabbia vide assisi in cerchio
i suoi compagni tutti volti al mare
tacitamente; e si godeano il sole,
e la primaverile brezza arguta
s'udian fischiare nelle bianche barbe.
Sedean come per uso i longiremi
vecchi compagni d'Odisseo sul lido,

XI. The Beached Ship

And the old poet and the old hero walked
the shoreline of the loud sea, reflecting
on much, and there, on the curve of the beach,
small and black, appeared their ship.
They saw the stern, its shadow looming
over the sand, though the sun wasn't very
high yet. And over it, noisy white seagulls
coasted, between the sea and the sky.
And the hero's eye saw that the pitch was still
fresh: and saw that the stones were lying
by its side, because the wind, calmed,
no longer made the ship shake; and saw,
in a row, hanging there, on the ship's side,
from the rigging, the cowhide ropes;
and saw the blades of the well-made
oars stick up from the watermark of the stern.
His heart smiled, for the ship was seaworthy
for the voyage; and he walked around her
like a swift charioteer around his chariot
before he yokes up his two horses.
He came to the prow with its red lead,
and on the sand he saw, seated in a circle,
all his companions, facing the sea,
silent, enjoying the sun; and they heard
the fresh spring breeze, a breeze that
whistled through their white beards.
They sat, as their custom was, on the beach,
these companions of the hero, Odysseus;

e da dieci anni lo attendean sul mare
col tempo bello e con la nuova aurora.
E veduta la rondine, le donne
recavano alla nave alte sul capo
l'anfore piene di fiammante vino
e pieni d'orzo triturato gli otri.
E prima che la nuova alba spargesse
le rose in cielo, essi veniano al mare,
i longiremi d'Odisseo compagni,
reggendo sopra il forte omero i remi,
ognuno il suo. Poi su la rena assisi
stavano, sotto la purpurea prora,
con gli occhi rossi a numerar le ondate,
ad ascoltarsi il vento nelle barbe,
ad ascoltare striduli gabbiani,
cantare in mare marinai lontani.
Poi quando il sole si tuffava e quando
sopra venia l'oscurità, ciascuno
prendeva il remo, ed alle sparse case
tornavan muti per le strade ombrate.

they had been waiting there for him for ten years,
in good weather and with each new dawn.
and seeing the swallow, a sign, their wives
brought to the ship, carried on their heads,
amphora filled with flaming wine, and goat-skins
filled with barley milled in a mortar.
And before the new spring dawn scattered
roses against the sky, they came down to the sea,
these longtime companions of Odysseus,
carrying their long oars on their shoulders,
each his own. Then they seated themselves
on the sand, under the red prow of lead,
with their eyes also red, counting the waves
as they broke, listening to the wind whistle
through their beards, hearing the piercing gulls,
and far off sailors singing far out to sea. When the
sun fell, when darkness covered everything;
they would take up their long oars and return,
silently, to their scattered homes,
walking through the shadows on the roads.

XII. Il timone

Ed ecco, appena il vecchio Eroe comparve
sorsero tutti, fermi in lui con gli occhi.
Come quando nel verno ispido i bovi
giacciono, avvinti, innanzi al lor presepe;
sdraiati a terra ruminano il pasto
povero, mentre frusciano l'acquate;
se con un fascio d'odoroso fieno
viene il bifolco, sorgono, pur lenta-
mente, né gli occhi stolgono dal fascio:
così sorsero i vecchi, ma nessuno
gli andava, stretto da pudor, più presso.
Ed egli, sotto il teschio irto del lupo,
così parlò tra lo sciacquìo del mare:
Compagni, udite ciò che il cuor mi chiede
sino da quando ritornai per sempre.
Per sempre? chiese, e, No, rispose il cuore.
Tornare, ei volle; terminar, non vuole.
Si desse, giunti alla lor selva, ai remi
barbàre in terra e verzicare abeti!
Ma no! Né può la nera nave al fischio
del vento dar la tonda ombra di pino.
E pur non vuole il rosichìo del tarlo,
ma l'ondata, ma il vento e l'uragano.
Anch'io la nube voglio, e non il fumo;
il vento, e non il sibilo del fuso,
non l'odïoso fuoco che sornacchia,
ma il cielo e il mare che risplende e canta.
Compagni, come il nostro mare io sono,

XII. The Rudder

And now, just as the old hero
appeared, they all rose, eyes fixed on him.
As when oxen, in the sharpness of winter,
lie down, tied, before their trough,
spread out on the ground, chewing their food,
humble, while the rain falls in heavy sheets;
if a peasant comes with a bundle
of sweet smelling hay, they rise, but slowly,
their eyes never losing sight of the bundle:
so these old men rose, but not one of them
approached the hero, for they were held back by awe.
And he, from beneath the scraggly skull of a wolf,
spoke this to them through the smashing of the waves:
"Companions, hear what my own heart asks
since the time that I returned at last forever.
'Forever?' I asked, and 'no,' answered my heart.
My heart wanted to return, but it did not want it all to end.
If the oars, far back in the woods, now root
themselves in the ground, there will be green fir trees
again. But no! The black ship cannot produce, as
the wind whistles, the shadow of the pine tree.
And the ship does not seek after gnawing
rot, but instead seeks waves, winds, storms.
And I too, want the clouds and not smoke
from a hearth, the wind and not the whirring spindle,
not the hateful hearth that spits and coughs,
but the sky and the sea that shine and sing.
Companions, I am just like our sea which is white

ch'è bianco all'orlo, ma cilestro in fondo.
Io non so che, lasciai, quando alla fune
diedi, lo stolto che pur fui, la scure;
nell'antro a mare ombrato da un gran lauro,
nei prati molli di viola e d'appio,
o dove erano cani d'oro a guardia,
immortalmente, della grande casa,
e dove uomini in forma di leoni
battean le lunghe code in veder noi,
o non so dove. E vi ritorno. Io vedo
che ciò che feci è già minor del vero.
Voi lo sapete, che portaste al lido
negli otri l'orzo triturato, e il vino
color di fiamma nel ben chiuso doglio,
che l'uno è sangue e l'altro a noi midollo.
E spalmaste la pece alla carena,
ch'è come l'olio per l'ignudo atleta;
e portaste le gomene che serpi
dormono in groppo o sibilano ai venti;
e toglieste le pietre, anche portaste
l'aerea vela; alla dormente nave,
che sempre sogna nel giacere in secco,
portaste ognun la vostra ala di remo;
e ora dunque alla ben fatta nave
che manca più, vecchi compagni? Al mare
la vecchia nave: amici, ecco il timone.
Così parlò tra il sussurrìo dell'onde.

at the shore and surface, but clear blue beneath it.
I could not know what I gave up, younger fool
that I was, when I put the axe to the rope;
in a cave by the sea shaded with laurel,
in the gentle fields of violet and anise,
where the golden dogs, immortal, stood
guard over the great house, and where
men, in the shape of lions lashed their long
tails whenever and wherever they saw us.
And so I'll return there.
Now I see how my deeds are less than true.
You know well, you who carried the crushed
barley in goat skins, and also the wine,
the color of flame, in tightly sealed casks,
for one is marrow, the other our own blood.
And those of you who painted the hull with pitch,
which is like oil for the naked athlete, and those who
carried the heavy ropes which are serpentine
sleeping in knots or hissing in the wind;
and those who cleared away the stones, and carried
the bilious sail; and each of you who carried
his winged oar to the sleeping black ship
that dreams forever when grounded.
And so now, my old companions, now—
what are we missing?
Let's sail it! Dear old companions, grab the rudder!"
    And so he spoke through the sea's murmuring.

XIII. La partenza

Ed ecco a tutti colorirsi il cuore
dell'azzurro color di lontananza;
e vi scorsero l'ombra del Ciclope
e v'udirono il canto della Maga:
l'uno parava sufolando al monte
pecore tante, quante sono l'onde;
l'altra tessea cantando l'immortale
sua tela così grande come il mare.
E tutti al mare trassero la nave
su travi tonde, come su le ruote;
e avvinsero gli ormeggi ad un lentisco
che verzicava sopra un erto scoglio;
e già salito, il vecchio Eroe nell'occhio
fece passar la barra del timone;
e stette in piedi sopra la pedagna.
Era seduto presso lui l'Aedo.
E con un cenno fece ai remiganti
salir la nave ed impugnare il remo.
Egli tagliò la fune con la scure.
E cantava un cuculo tra le fronde,
cantava nella vigna un potatore,
passava un gregge lungo su la rena
con incessante gemere d'agnelli,
ricciute donne in lavatoi perenni
batteano a gara i panni alto cianciando
e dalle case d'Itaca rupestre
balzava in alto il fumo mattutino.
E i marinai seduti alle scalmiere

XIII. The Departure

And so we see how the heart dreams everything
with the blue color of distance and memory;
how it shortens the shadow of the Cyclops
and hears the far-off song of the Sorceress:
the one appears to guard so many sheep
on the hillside, as many as there are waves;
the other seems to weave an immortal song
on a canvas that stretches over the wide ocean.
    And they all dragged the ship down to the sea
on circular beams as though it were on wheels;
and they tied the mooring to a mastic tree
that turned green at the top of a steep incline;
the old hero had already gone on board.
He passed the tiller on to the helmsman;
and he planted his feet in front of the stretcher.
Aedo, the poet, was seated very close to him.
And with a gesture he signaled the oarsmen
to climb into the ship and take up their oars.
Odysseus cut the cable free with the axe.
And a cuckoo sang a song in the bushes.
a farmer sang while he pruned his vineyard,
a flock of sheep passed on the sands of the beach,
with an incessant mewling of tiny lambs,
curly-haired women washed their endless laundry,
pounding the clothes as rivals gossiped out loud
and from the rocky houses of Ithaca
the early morning hearth fires leapt to the sky.
And the sailors seated at the ship's oarlocks

facean coi remi biancheggiar il flutto.
E Femio vide sopra un alto groppo
di cavi attorti la vocal sua cetra,
la cetra ch'egli avea gittata, e un vecchio
dagli occhi rossi lieto avea raccolta
e portata alla nave, ai suoi compagni;
ed era a tutti, l'aurea cetra, a cuore,
come a bambino infante un rondinotto
morto, che così morto egli carezza
lieve con dita inabili e gli parla,
e teme e spera che gli prenda il volo.
E Femio prese la sua cetra, e lieve
la toccò, poi, forte intonò la voga
ai remiganti. E quell'arguto squillo
svegliò nel cuore immemore dei vecchi
canti sopiti; e curvi sopra i remi
cantarono con rauche esili voci.
- Ecco la rondine! Ecco la rondine! Apri!
ch'ella ti porta il bel tempo, i belli anni.
È nera sopra, ed il suo petto è bianco.
È venuta da uno che può tanto.
Oh! apriti da te, uscio di casa,
ch'entri costì la pace e l'abbondanza,
e il vino dentro il doglio da sé vada
e il pane d'orzo empia da sé la madia.
Uno anc'a noi, col sesamo, puoi darne!
Presto, ché non siam qui per albergare.
Apri, ché sto su l'uscio a piedi nudi!
Apri, ché non siam vecchi ma fanciulli! -

were making the waves billow white with their oars.
    And Femius saw, at the top of a knot
of twisted ropes, the lyre he had thrown out, found
by an old man with tears of joy in his eyes,
who brought it aboard and told his companions
it was for all a golden lyre of the heart,
the way a child mourns for a dead swallow
which, though he knows it is dead, caresses it,
with his clumsy fingers, and speaks softly
to it, both fearing and hoping it would take flight.
And Femius took up his lyre and touched it
lightly, and then he began to play loudly
to the oarsmen. How that sudden keen song
stirred the closed and forgotten hearts of those men!
They remembered sweet music and bent to the oars,
while singing out in their thin, raspy voices:
Here is the swallow! Here is the swallow! Open—
so she may bring us good weather, good years.
She is black on top and her breast is white.
She has come from one who is all powerful.
Open yourself to her, door of the house, so
she may enter, bringing peace and abundance,
and wine to make your sorrow disappear, and
barley bread to fill up all your breadboxes.
Some bread for us, too, with sesame!
Right now, so we won't have to stay here.
Open, so I seem to stand at my door with bare feet!
Open, so we won't be old men but young boys.

XIV. Il pitocco

Cantavano; e il lor canto era fanciullo,
dei tempi andati; non sapean che quello.
E nella stiva in cui giaceva immerso
nel dolce sonno, si stirò le braccia
e si sfregò le palpebre coi pugni
Iro, il pitocco. E niuno lo sapeva
laggiù, qual grosso baco che si chiude
in un irsuto bozzolo lanoso,
forse a dormire. Ché solea nel verno
lì nella nave d'Odisseo dormire,
se lo cacciava dalla calda stalla
l'uomo bifolco, o s'ei temeva i cani
del pecoraio. Nella buona estate
dormia sotto le stelle alla rugiada.
Ora quivi obliava la vecchiaia trista
e la fame; quando il suono e il canto
lo destò. Dentro gli ondeggiava il cuore:
Non odo il suono della cetra arguta?
Dunque non era sogno il mio, che or ora
portavo ai proci, ai proci morti, un messo:
ed ecco nell'opaco atrio la cetra
udivo, e le lor voci esili e rauche.
Invero udiva il tintinnio tuttora
e il canto fioco tra il fragor dell'onde,
qual di querule querule ranelle
per un'acquata, quando ancor c'è il sole.
E tra sé favellava Iro il pitocco:
O son presso ad un vero atrio di vivi?

XIV. The Beggar

They sang; and their song was a song of lost
youth, a song of times gone by; a time they couldn't
remember. And in the cargo hold in which he lay sunk
deep in a sweet slumber, Iro, the beggar, stretched
his arms and rubbed his eyelids with his fists. And no one
knew that down in the hold this big caterpillar had closed
itself into a wooly cocoon, perhaps just to sleep. There,
inside the ship of Odysseus, Iro wintered; banished
from the warm stable by the plowman, as usual,
and by the persistent dogs of the shepherd.
At the height of summer, he slept under the stars
on the dewy ground. Then he would forget the sadness
of old age and of hunger; but when the music and song
stirred him, great waves tossed inside his heart:
     "Did I hear the music from a golden lyre?
Then it wasn't a dream that now, at this very hour,
messengers brought word the dead suitors,
and so I think I heard the golden lyre in the dark hall—
and their voices, frail and hoarse."
     He clearly heard the continuous tinkling and
the faint song between the roaring of the waves, like
that of the peevish whine of tree frogs, in a downpour
while the sun still shone. And he spoke to himself,
this Iro the beggar:
     "O, is this an entrance hall of the living?

e forse alcuno mi tirò pel piede
sino al cortile, poi che la mascella
sotto l'orecchio mi fiaccò col pugno?
Come altra volta, che Odisseo divino
lottò con Iro, malvestiti entrambi.
Così pensando si rizzò sui piedi
e su le mani, e gli fiottava il capo,
e movendo traballava come ebbro
di molto vino; e ad Odisseo comparve,
nuotando a vuoto, ed ai remigatori,
terribile. Ecco e s'interruppe il canto,
e i remi alzati non ripreser l'acqua,
e la nave da prua si drizzò, come
cavallo indomito, e lanciò supino,
a piè di Femio e d'Odisseo seduti,
Iro il pitocco. E lo conobbe ognuno
quando, abbrancati i lor ginocchi, sorse
inginocchioni, e gli grondava il sangue
giù per il mento dalle labbra e il naso.
E un dolce riso si levò di tutti,
alto, infinito. Ed egli allor comprese,
e vide dileguare Itaca, e vide
sparir le case, onde balzava il fumo:
e le due coscie si percosse e pianse.
E sorridendo il vecchio Eroe gli disse:
Soffri. Hai qui tetto e letto, e orzo e vino.
Sii nella nave il dispensier del cibo,
e bevi e mangia e dormi, Iro non-Iro.

And will someone then pull me by my feet
into the courtyard, and afterwards will
they box my ears into my jawbone with their fists,
like the other time, when the ragtag Iro fought with
the divine Odysseus?"
    And thinking all this, he pulled himself onto
his feet, his head reeling, and when he moved
he staggered forward like he'd been drinking
too much wine; he appeared to Odysseus and the oarsmen,
a terrifying sight, swimming in the darkness. They
stopped singing and raised the oars.
    When the rowing stopped, the ship reared up
its prow like a wild horse, throwing Iro the beggar
at the feet of the seated Femius and Odysseus.
And everyone recognized him when he fell, clutching
at their knees, laughing, blood pouring from his lips
and nose down to his chin. And then sweet laughter
rose from all of them, endless laughter. In this way
he understood that he was looking at the scattered
Ithacans, and he saw the houses disappear, the waves
dissolve into vapor; he slapped his thighs and wept.
    And laughing, the old hero said to him, "Have
patience, here you have a bed and a roof and barley
and wine. Be food steward on board ship, and drink
and eat and sleep, Iro, not-Iro."

XV. La procella

E sopra il flutto nove dì la nave
corse sospinta dal remeggio alato,
e notte e giorno, ché Odisseo due schiere
dinumerò degl'incliti compagni;
e l'una al sonno e l'altra era alla voga.
Nel decimo l'aurora mattiniera
a un lieve vento dispergea le rose.
Ei dalla scassa l'albero d'abete
levò, lo congegnò dentro la mastra,
e con drizze di cuoio alzò la vela,
ben torto, e saldi avvinse alle caviglie
di prua gli stragli, ma di poppa i bracci.
E il vento urtò la vela in mezzo, e il flutto
rumoreggiava intorno alla carena.
E legarono allora anche le scotte
lungo la nave che correa veloce:
e pose in mezzo un'anfora di vino
Iro il pitocco, ed arrancando intorno
lo ministrava ai marinai seduti;
e sorse un riso. E nove dì sul flutto
li resse in corsa il vento e il timoniere.
Nel decimo tra nubi era l'aurora,
e venne notte, ed una aspra procella
tre quattro strappi fece nella vela;
e il Laertiade ammainò la vela,
e disse a tutti di gettarsi ai remi;
ed essi curvi sopra sé di forza
remigavano. E nove dì sbalzati

XV. The Storm

And the ship sailed for nine days above the waves,
its course hastened night and day by winged oars,
for Odysseus had broken the famed crew
into two groups of ten, and one group slept
while the other took the oars. At dawn of
the tenth day a soft wind scattered roses
in the sky. He lifted a spruce from the deck
and, setting it into the mast hole,
he contrived a device to raise the crooked sail
with a leather halyard, and drew the bow stays
taut around the pins on the wing of the stern.
The wind tore the sail in half and the waves
crashed around the hull of the boat. So they
tied sheets the length of the swift-running ship:
and in the middle of the deck Iro, the Beggar,
set an amphora of wine, cut into it with
a bill-hook and distributed the contents,
bringing laughter to the seated mariners.
And for nine days upon the waves, both pilot
and wind kept on course. On the tenth, dawn broke
through clouds and when night came a violent storm
made three or four tears in the sail; and Odysseus
lowered the sail and ordered them all to rush
to oars; and they bent themselves to hard rowing.
And for nine days they moved backwards against
the waves in deadly winds. At last, at nightfall,
the winds and waves calmed, and they saw shore.
At this, the old hero pushed the ship forward

eran dai flutti e da funesti venti.
Infine i venti rappaciati e i flutti,
sul far di sera, videro una spiaggia.
A quella spinse il vecchio Eroe la nave,
in un seno tranquillo come un letto.
E domati da sonno e da stanchezza,
dormian sul lido, ove batteva l'onda.
Ma non dormiva egli, Odisseo, pur vinto
dalla stanchezza. Ché pensava in cuore
d'essere giunto all'isola di Circe:
vedea la casa di pulite pietre,
come in un sogno, e sorgere leoni
lenti, e le rosse bocche allo sbadiglio
aprire, e un poco già scodinzolare;
e risonava il grande atrio del canto
di tessitrice. Ora Odisseo parlava:
Terpiade Femio, dormi? Odimi: il sogno
dolce e dimenticato ecco io risogno!
Era l'amore; ch'ora mi sommuove,
come procella omai finita, il cuore.
Diceva; e nella notte alta e serena
dormiva il vento, e vi sorgea la falce,
su macchie e selve, della bianca luna
già presso al fine, e s'effondea l'olezzo
di grandi aperti calici di fiori
non mai veduti. Ed il gran mare ancora
si ricordava, e con le lunghe ondate
bianche di schiuma singhiozzava al lido.

into a bay calm as a bed. And they, overpowered
by weariness, slept on the beach, pounded by waves.

   But Odysseus did not sleep, though he was
overcome by exhaustion. He believed in his heart
they had arrived at Circe's island: he saw
the house of polished stone as though in a dream,
and the waking of sleepy lions, their red mouths
in open yawns, their tails beginning to slash,
and the great atrium resounding with the song
of the Weaver. Now Odysseus spoke:
   "Terpius, Femius, are you asleep?
Listen to me: the sweet and forgotten dream is
moving inside me! It is love that is
stirring me now, like a storm almost over."

   And that's what he said; and in the deep
calm night the wind slept, and the pale sickle
moon finally rose in nearby woods and forests,
carrying the perfume of great open cups
of flowers which never had or would be seen.
And the great sea remembered him again, and with long
white surges, it heaved its sobbing foam upon the shore.

XVI. L'isola Eea

E con la luce rosea dell'aurora
s'avvide, ch'era l'isola di Circe.
E disse a Femio, al molto caro Aedo:
Terpiade Femio, vieni a me compagno
con la tua cetra, ch'ella oda il tuo canto
mortale, e tu l'eterno inno ne apprenda.
E disse ad Iro, dispensier del cibo:
Con gli altri presso il grigio mar tu resta,
e mangia e bevi, ch'ella non ti batta
con la sua verga, e n'abbi poi la ghianda
per cibo, e pianga, sgretolando il cibo,
con altra voce, o Iro non-più-Iro.
Così diceva sorridendo, e mosse
col dolce Aedo, per le macchie e i boschi,
e vide il passo donde l'alto cervo
d'arboree corna era disceso a bere:
Ma non vide la casa alta di Circe.
Or a lui disse il molto caro Aedo:
C'è addietro. Una tempesta è il desiderio,
ch'agli occhi è nube quando ai piedi è vento.
Ma il luogo egli conobbe, ove gli occorse
il dio che salva, e riconobbe il poggio
donde strappò la buona erba, che nera
ha la radice, e come latte il fiore.
E non vide la casa alta di Circe.
Or a lui disse il molto caro Aedo:
C'è innanzi. La vecchiezza è una gran calma,
che molto stanca, ma non molto avanza.

XVI. THE ISLAND OF AEAEA

And with the rosy light of dawn
the island of Circe appeared to him.
And Odysseus said to Femius the bard, son of Terpius,
"Greatly esteemed poet, come accompany me on
your lyre, so the goddess can hear your song of mortality,
and you can teach us her song of immortality."
    He said to Iro, his steward of food supplies,
"You and the others stay close to the gray sea.
Eat and drink, she cannot touch you with her wand.
Eat no more acorns and break your food in pieces,
weeping in another voice, Iro not-Iro."
    He said this smiling, and moving through
the woods and brush with the sweet poet,
and he saw the pass where the tall stag, with horns
like branches, came down the slope to drink.
But he did not see the tall house of Circe.
    So he said to the highly esteemed poet,
"It is there, in back of us. A storm that we wished for,
giving wind to our feet but misting over our eyes."
    He knew the place where the god Hermes
confronted him, and he recognized the little hill
where he could dig up the right herb,
the one with black roots and a flower like milk.
He didn't see the tall house of Circe.
    So the highly esteemed poet said,
"It is there, in front of us. Old age brings steady
nerves if you are tired and it is not too advanced."

E proseguì pei monti e per le valli,
e selve e boschi, attento s'egli udisse
lunghi sbadigli di leoni, désti
al lor passaggio, o l'immortal canzone
di tessitrice, della dea vocale.
E nulla udì nell'isola deserta,
e nulla vide; e si tuffava il sole,
e la stellata oscurità discese.
E l'Eroe disse al molto caro Aedo:
Troppo nel cielo sono alte le stelle,
perché la strada io possa ormai vedere.
Or qui dormiamo, ed assai caldo il letto
a noi facciamo; ché risorto è il vento.
Disse, e ambedue si giacquero tra molte
foglie cadute, che ammucchiate al tronco
di vecchie quercie aveva la procella;
e parvero nel mucchio, essi, due tizzi,
vecchi, riposti con un po' di fuoco,
sotto la grigia cenere infeconda.
E sopra loro alta stormìa la selva.
Ed ecco il cuore dell'Eroe leoni
udì ruggire. Avean dormito il giorno,
certo, e l'eccelsa casa era vicina.
Invero intese anche la voce arguta,
in lontananza, della dea, che, sola,
non prendea sonno e ancor tessea notturna.
Né prendea sonno egli, Odisseo, ma spesso
si volgea su le foglie stridule aspre.

And they continued through mountains and valleys,
through woods and forest, alert to the sound
of the yawns of lions awakened by their passing,
or the immortal song of the weaver, the singing goddess.
And he heard nothing on the deserted island,
nor did he see anything move. And the sun plunged
from the sky and a star-filled darkness fell.
    And the hero said to the greatly
esteemed poet, "The stars are too high in the heavens
for me to see the way from now on. So let us
sleep here, and the bed we make will be cold,
since the wind has risen again."
    He said this and they both lay down
among the many fallen leaves heaped around
the trunk of the ancient oaks during the storm.
And in the pile of leaves there appeared two
smoking embers, old, but still alive, and
with a little bit of fire left in the dead gray ash.
And here the heart of the hero heard a roar
of lions that slept in the daytime,
so surely, they could sense,
the house was very close. This feeling was
made more certain by the clear voice
in the distance of the goddess who, alone,
never went to sleep, but wove all night.
    Nor did he, Odysseus, go to sleep at all, but he tossed
and turned the whole night in his rough bed of leaves.

XVII. L'AMORE

E con la luce rosea dell'aurora
non udì più ruggito di leoni,
che stanchi alfine di vegliar, col muso
dormian disteso su le lunghe zampe.
Dormiva anch'ella, allo smorir dell'alba,
pallida e scinta sopra il noto letto.
E il vecchio Eroe parlava al vecchio Aedo:
Prenda ciascuno una sua via: ch'è meglio.
Ma diamo un segno; con la cetra, Aedo,
tu, che ritrova pur da lungi il cuore.
Ma s'io ritrovi ciò che il cuor mi vuole,
ti getto allora un alalà di guerra,
quale gettavo nella mischia orrenda
eroe di bronzo sopra i morti ignudi,
io; che il cuore lo intenda anche da lungi.
Disse, e taceva dei leoni uditi
nell'alta notte, e della dea canora.
E prese ognuno la sua via diversa
per macchie e boschi, e monti e valli, e nulla
udì l'Eroe, se non ruggir le quercie
a qualche rara raffica, e cantare
lontan lontano eternamente il mare.
E non vide la casa, né i leoni
dormir col muso su le lunghe zampe,
né la sua dea. Ma declinava il sole,
e tutte già s'ombravano le strade.
E mise allora un alalà di guerra
per ritrovare il vecchio Aedo, almeno;

XVII. Love

    With the rosy light of the dawn,
the roaring of the lions who, weary at last,
slept with their muzzles stretched out
along their paws, was no longer heard.
The goddess also, pale herself, slept alone
in the well-known bed, as dawn grew lighter.
And the old hero spoke to the old poet:
    "Everyone has his own life; that's it.
But I will give a sign; with the lyre, poet,
to you who keep a pure heart at a distance.
But if I find again what my heart wishes for,
I will send you a sign of war, as once I did,
which means I will have thrown myself again
into a horrendous fray, and that I, the hero
of bronze stand above the naked dead: that
your heart will understand, even at a distance."
    So he spoke, and the silence of the lions
and the goddess was all one heard in the dead
of night.
    And each one went his own way, through
woods and forests, mountains and valleys, and the hero
heard nothing, unless it was an odd squall roaring
in the oaks, or the eternal, distant song, of the sea.
And he did not see the house, or the lions asleep
with their muzzles on their paws, or his own goddess.
But the sun is setting and already all the routes
are shadowed. He had sent forth a sign of war
to bring back to the old poet; and listened closely

e porse attento ad ogni aura l'orecchio
se udisse almeno della cetra il canto;
e sì, l'udì; traendo a lei, l'udiva,
sempre più mesta, sempre più soave,
cantar l'amore che dormia nel cuore,
e che destato solo allor ti muore.
La udì più presso, e non la vide, e vide
nel folto mucchio delle foglie secche
morto l'Aedo; e forse ora, movendo
pel cammino invisibile, tra i pioppi
e i salici che gettano il lor frutto,
toccava ancora con le morte dita
l'eburnea cetra: così mesto il canto
n'era, e così lontano e così vano.
Ma era in alto, a un ramo della quercia,
la cetra arguta, ove l'avea sospesa
Femio, morendo, a che l'Eroe chiamasse
brillando al sole o tintinnando al vento:
al vento che scotea gli alberi, al vento
che portava il singulto ermo del mare.
E l'Eroe pianse, e s'avviò notturno
alla sua nave, abbandonando morto
il dolce Aedo, sopra cui moveva
le foglie secche e l'aurea cetra il vento.

to any sound the ear might hear, and heard at last
the song of the lyre; yes, heard it; heard it,
as he approached, always sadder, always sweeter,
to sing of love that sleeps in the heart. The sound
came closer, but he sees nothing, then sees in the thick
heap of dead leaves, the dead poet; now moving along
the surface invisibly, among poplars and willows
that give him their fruits, and the dead fingers
that touch the lyre again: the wind: so the song
will be sad and far away and empty. But high up,
there was the branch of an oak, the perfect lyre,
in which the notes will hang, where Femius,
dying, placed it, to cry out to the hero, to the sun
shining, and the wind singing; to the wind which
shortens trees, to the wind which carried a single
sob from the sea. And the hero cried, as night began
on the ship, after he had abandoned the dead, sweet poet,
above whom the wind moved dry leaves and a golden lyre.

XVIII. L'isola delle capre

Indi più lungi navigò, più triste,
E corse i flutti nove di la nave
or col remeggio or con la bianca vela.
E giunse alfine all'isola selvaggia
ch'è senza genti e capre sole alleva.
E qui vinti da sonno e da stanchezza
dormian sul lido a cui batteva l'onda.
Ma con la luce rosea dell'aurora
vide Odisseo la terra dei Ciclopi,
non presso o lungi, e gli sovvenne il vanto
ch'ei riportò con la sua forza e il senno,
del mangiatore d'uomini gigante.
Ed oblioso egli cercò l'Aedo
per dire a lui: Terpiade Femio, il sogno
dolce e dimenticato io lo risogno:
era la gloria . . . Ma il vocale Aedo
dormia sotto le stridule aspre foglie,
e la sua tetra là cantava al vento
il dolce amore addormentato in cuore,
che appena desto solo allor ti muore.
E l'Eroe disse ai vecchi remiganti:
Compagni, udite. Qui non son che capre;
e qui potremmo d'infinita carne
empirci, fino a che sparisca il sole.
Ma no: le voglio prendere al pastore,
pecore e capre; ch'è, così, ben meglio.
È là, pari a un cocuzzolo silvestro,
quel mio pastore. Io l'accecai. Ma il grande

XVIII. Island of the Goats

Afterwards they sailed further and sadder.
And for nine days traveled over the waves,
now with oars, now with a full white sail.
They finally arrived at a wild island,
without any people, that fed only goats.
Overcome by sleep and fatigue,
they slept on a beach battered by waves.
    But with the rosy light of dawn
Odysseus saw the land of the Cyclops—
not very near nor far away—and it reminded
him of the boast he made to the gigantic
man-eater about his strength and cleverness.
But forgetting this, he sought the poet,
to tell him,
    "Terpius, Femius, I have dreamed
again the sweet forgotten dream, the one
about glory." The expressive poet
was asleep on the harsh rustling leaves,
and his sadness sang to the wind
about sweet love sleeping in one's
heart that leaves as soon as it is awakened.
The hero said to his old oarsmen:
"Comrades, listen. There's nothing
here but goats; and we could fill ourselves
up on meat until the sun goes down.
But no—I want to take from the shepherd
the sheep and the goats. This would be better."
The crown of a rustic hat appeared,
that of the shepherd. "I blinded him. But

cuor non m'è pago. Egli implorò dal padre,
ch'io perdessi al ritorno i miei compagni,
e mal tornassi, e in nave d'altri, e tardi.
Or sappia che ho compagni e che ritorno
sopra nave ben mia dal mio ritorno.
Andiamo: a mare troveremo un antro
tutto coperto, io ben lo so, di lauro.
Avessi ancora il mio divino Aedo!
Vorrei che il canto d'Odisseo là dentro
cantasse, e quegli nel tornare all'antro
sostasse cieco ad ascoltar quel canto,
coi greggi attorno, il mento sopra il pino.
E io sedessi all'ombra sua, nel lido!
Disse, e ai compagni longiremi ingiunse
di salir essi e sciogliere gli ormeggi.
Salirono essi, e in fila alle scalmiere
facean coi remi biancheggiare il flutto.
E giunti presso, videro sul mare,
in una punta, l'antro, alto, coperto
di molto lauro, e v'era intorno il chiuso
di rozzi blocchi, e lunghi pini e quercie
altochiomanti. E il vecchio Eroe parlava:
Là prendiam terra, ch'egli dal remeggio
non ci avvisti; ch'a gli orbi occhio è l'orecchio;
e non ci avventi un masso, come quello
che troncò in cima di quel picco nero,
e ci scagliò. Rimbombò l'onda al colpo.
Ed accennava un alto monte, tronco
del capo, che sorgeva solitario.

that great heart has not paid me back. He
implored the father for me to lose my comrades
in the return journey, for me to sail badly and
in the boats of others, and late. Now he knows
that I have comrades, that I am sailing
in my own ship, on my return. So, let's
go: at the sea we shall find a cave
I know well, all covered in laurel.
If only I still had my divine poet!
I would like the song of Odysseus
to be sung inside the cave, so that
when the Cyclops, so huge his chin
rests on the top of pines, enters
the cave he will remain in the dark listening
to this song, with the flocks all around,
and I will sit in the shade on the beach."
    He said this, telling his patient
comrades to go untie the mooring.
Then they got on board, lined up
at the oarlocks, making white-caps
with their oars. They arrived quickly,
going by sea, to the top of the deep cave
covered with laurel and hidden inside
by a rough covering of tall pines
and oaks which seemed like long
flowing hair. The old hero spoke again,
    "So then, let us land right
here, so he won't see us approach

by rowing, only this boulder which
cut off the top of this dark hill but,
with only the orbs of his eyes and
his sense of smell, he won't
attack us as before when a breaking
wave crashed against the bow."
   Then he showed them the tall
mountain cut off at the top, that rose by itself.

XIX. Il Ciclope

Ecco: ai compagni disse di restare
presso la nave e di guardar la nave.
Ed egli all'antro già movea, soletto,
per lui vedere non veduto, quando
parasse i greggi sufolando al monte.
Ora all'Eroe parlava Iro il pitocco:
Ben verrei reco per veder quell'uomo
che tanto mangia, e portar via, se posso,
di sui cannicci, già scolati i caci,
e qualche agnello dai gremiti stabbi.
Poi ch'Iro ha fame. E s'ei dentro ci fosse,
il gran Ciclope, sai ch'Iro è veloce
ben che non forte; è come Iri del cielo
che va sul vento con il piè di vento.
L'Eroe sorrise, e insieme i due movendo,
il pitocco e l'Eroe, giunsero all'antro.
Dentro e' non era. Egli pasceva al monte
i pingui greggi. E i due meravigliando
vedean graticci pieni di formaggi,
e gremiti d'agnelli e di capretti
gli stabbi, e separati erano, ognuni
ne' loro, i primaticci, i mezzanelli
e i serotini. E d'uno dei recinti
ecco che uscì, con alla poppa il bimbo,
un'altocinta femmina, che disse:
Ospiti, gioia sia con voi. Chi siete?
donde venuti? a cambiar qui, qual merce?
Ma l'uomo è fuori, con la greggia, al monte;
tra poco torna, ché già brucia il sole.

XIX. The Cyclops

So: he told his companions to stay
near the ship and to watch over it. And he
had already moved toward the cave, alone,
to see the Cyclops but not be seen, as
the shining flocks covered the mountain.
Then Iro the beggar spoke to the hero:
  "I would really like to see that man
who eats so much, and to carry away, if I can,
some intestines, already cleaned, for sausage,
and some lamb to stuff it full. For your
Iro is hungry. And if the great Cyclops is
within the cave, you know Iro is very fast
though not very brave, and like the angry sky
that comes, he flees on foot with the wind."
  The hero smiled, and the two of them climbed,
the beggar and the hero, until they reached the cave.
Cyclops wasn't there. They went up the mountain
covered with flocks. And the two of them marveled
at seeing baskets filled with cheeses and
overflowing with lamb and with goatskins,
also filled, and everything was laid out, everything
was there, first courses, middle courses,
later courses. And from one of the fences
that stood there, with a child to her breast,
there was a high-waisted woman, who said:
  "Guests, be joyful. Who are you?
Where are you from? Are you here to trade?"
But the hero, beyond the fence, with the beggar,
glanced around at food already baking in the sun.

Ma pur mangiate, se il tardar v'è noia.
Sorrise ad Iro il vecchio Eroe: poi disse:
Ospite donna, e pur con te sia gioia.
Ma dunque l'uomo a venerare apprese
gli dei beati, ed ora sa la legge,
benché tuttora abiti le spelonche,
come i suoi pari, per lo scabro monte?
E l'altocinta femmina rispose:
Ospite, ognuno alla sua casa è legge,
e della moglie e de' suoi nati è re.
Ma noi non deprediamo altri: ben altri,
ch'errano in vano su le nere navi,
come ladroni, a noi pecore o capre
hanno predate. Altrui portando il male
rischian essi la vita. Ma voi siete
vecchi, e cercate un dono qui, non prede.
Verso Iro il vecchio anche ammiccò: poi disse:
Ospite donna, ben di lui conosco
quale sia l'ospitale ultimo dono.
Ed ecco un grande tremulo belato
s'udì venire, e un suono di zampogna,
e sufolare a pecore sbandate:
e ne' lor chiusi si levò più forte
il vagir degli agnelli e dei capretti.
Ch'egli veniva, e con fragore immenso
depose un grande carico di selva
fuori dell'antro: e ne rintronò l'antro.
E Iro in fondo s'appiattò tremando.

If the meal was already eaten, and we are too late,
it would be rude to ask to be fed.
    Smiling to Iro, the old hero says:
"Hostess, equal joy also to you.
But how should a man, approaching, honor
these lucky men, and to know now their customs,
because they always live in a cave
and leave their tracks on the rough mountain."
    And the high-waisted woman responded:
"Guest, everyone is the law in his own house,
and of his wife, and his children and possessions.
But we do not plunder others; yet those
on the black ships who were too proud,
like thieves, have plundered our sheep,
our goats. Others think only evil and so
they risk their lives. But you are
old, and seek a gift, not plunder."
    The old hero winked at Iro, then said:
"Hostess, I know him well, this Cyclops,
and as the host he should find me a gift."
    And at this they heard a great trembling
and bleating approaching, and a sound of bagpipes.
And trembling, the black sheep scatter,
and no force can hold back
the cry of the sheep and the goats.
And then Cyclops with a great crash,
dropped an enormous bundle of wood
outside, and thundered into the cave.
And Iro hid, shaking, on the ground.

XX. La gloria

E l'uomo entrò, ma l'altocinta donna
gli venne incontro, e lo seguiano i figli
molti, e le molte pecore e le capre
l'una all'altra addossate erano impaccio,
per arrivare ai piccoli. E infinito
era il belato, e l'alte grida, e il fischio.
Ma in breve tacque il gemito, e ciascuno
suggea scodinzolando la sua poppa.
E l'uomo vide il vecchio Eroe che in cuore
meravigliava ch'egli fosse un uomo;
e gli parlò con le parole alate:
Ospite, mangia. Assai per te ne abbiamo.
Ed al pastore il vecchio Eroe rispose:
Ospite, dimmi. Io venni di lontano,
molto lontano; eppur io già, dal canto
d'erranti aedi, conoscea quest'antro.
Io sapea d'un enorme uomo gigante
che vivea tra infinite greggie bianche,
selvaggiamente, qui su i monti, solo
come un gran picco; con un occhio tondo...
Ed il pastore al vecchio Eroe rispose:
Venni di dentro terra, io, da molt'anni;
e nulla seppi d'uomini giganti.
E l'Eroe riprendeva, ed i fanciulli
gli erano attorno, del pastore, attenti:
che aveva solo un occhio tondo, in fronte,
come uno scudo bronzeo, come il sole,
acceso, vuoto. Verga un pino gli era,
e gli era il sommo d'un gran monte, pietra

XX. Fame

The man entered, and the high-waisted woman
came toward him, followed by many sons,
and by many sheep and goats
pushing against each other making it hard
for the small ones. But finally,
with bleats and cries, a great clamor,
each one found and sucked
its own mother's teats, wagging its tail.
    And the man saw the old hero and wondered
secretly if this was the famous Odysseus;
and spoke to him in winged words:
"Welcome, eat. We don't have much to offer you."
    And to the shepherd, the old hero responds:
"Thank you, humble one. I come from far away,
too far away; still, I already know,
from the song of the wandering poets,
about this cave. I know all about
a great giant of a man who lived
savagely with an extraordinary white herd,
who came alone over the mountains,
like a great peak himself, with a round eye . . ."
    And the shepherd answered the old hero:
"I came from within the earth myself, many years ago;
and saw nothing of a gigantic man."
    And the hero resumed, while young men
stood around the shepherd, listening:
"This one had only one round eye, on his forehead,
like a bronze shield, like the sun,

da fionda, e in mare li scagliava, e tutto
bombiva il mare al loro piombar giù...
Ed il pastore, tra i suoi pastorelli,
pensava, e disse all'altocinta moglie:
Non forse è questo che dicea tuo padre?
Che un savio c'era, uomo assai buono e grande
per qui, Telemo Eurymide, che vecchio
dicea che in mare piovea pietre, un tempo,
sì, da quel monte, che tra gli altri monti
era più grande; e che s'udian rimbombi
nell'alta notte, e che appariva un occhio
nella sua cima, un tondo occhio di fuoco . . .
Ed al pastore chiese il moltaccorto:
E l'occhio a lui chi trivellò notturno?
Ed il pastore ad Odisseo rispose:
Al monte? l'occhio? trivellò? Nessuno.
Ma nulla io vidi, e niente udii. Per nave
ci vien talvolta, e non altronde, il male.
Disse: e dal fondo Iro avanzò, che disse:
Tu non hai che fanciulli per aiuto.
Prendi me, ben sì vecchio, ma nessuno
veloce ha il piede più di me, se debbo
cercar l'agnello o rintracciare il becco.
Per chi non ebbe un tetto mai, pastore,
quest'antro è buono. Io ti sarò garzone.

inflamed and empty. There was a pine log
for a catapult, the highest of the mountains made
a stone, and he hurled it into the sea
which resounded with an enormous crash."
    But the shepherd, with all of the other shepherds,
considered, and said to his wife:
"Maybe this is what your father was talking about?
He was a wise man, as good and as grand
as you, Telemo Eurymide's son, an old prophet
who said that stones once rained into the sea,
from the mountain that was the highest
of all of the mountains; and the booming
was heard during the whole night, and on its
peak, an eye would appear, round and full of fire."
    And the shepherd told him to be quick:
"And his eye, who put it out in the night with a stake?
    And the shepherd replied to Odysseus:
"On a mountain? An eye? A stake? No.
I have never heard or seen anything. Sometimes a ship
comes from somewhere else, but not bringing trouble."
    He spoke: and from the background, Iro came
forward:
"You do not have young men to help you.
Take me, I'm well, if old, and no one
has faster feet than I do, when I have to
search for the lamb and chase after the goat.
For a shepherd who's never had shelter,
a cave is good. I will be your assistant."

XXI. Le Sirene

ndi più lungi navigò, più triste.
E stando a poppa il vecchio Eroe guardava
scuro verso la terra de' Ciclopi,
e vide dal cocuzzolo selvaggio
del monte, che in disparte era degli altri,
levarsi su nel roseo cielo un fumo,
tenue, leggiero, quale esce su l'alba
dal fuoco che al pastore arse la notte.
Ma i remiganti curvi sopra i remi
vedeano, sì, nel violaceo mare
lunghe tremare l'ombre dei Ciclopi
fermi sul lido come ispidi monti.
E il cuore intanto ad Odisseo vegliardo
squittiva dentro, come cane in sogno:
Il mio sogno non era altro che sogno;
e vento e fumo. Ma sol buono è il vero.
E gli sovvenne delle due Sirene.
C'era un prato di fiori in mezzo al mare.
Nella gran calma le ascoltò cantare:
Ferma la nave! Odi le due Sirene
ch'hanno la voce come è dolce il miele;
ché niuno passa su la nave nera
che non si fermi ad ascoltarci appena,
e non ci ascolta, che non goda al canto,
né se ne va senza saper più tanto:
ché noi sappiamo tutto quanto avviene
sopra la terra dove è tanta gente!
Gli sovveniva, e ripensò che Circe

XXI. THE SIRENS

After a long voyage, more sadness.
And the old hero looked out from the stern
toward the dark land of the Cyclops,
and saw from the summit of the wild
mountain, set apart from all the others,
smoke rising into a rosy sky,
like the smoke that rises from
a fire some shepherd has burned all night.
But the oarsmen bent over their oars,
seeing, for themselves, in the violet sea,
the long trembling shadow of the Cyclops,
motionless on shore like a forbidden mountain.
And meanwhile the old heart of venerable Odysseus
yelped inside him, like dogs in dreaming:
    "My dream was like no other dream;
it was wind and smoke. But truth is the only good thing."
    And the two Sirens can help with this. There was
a meadow of flowers in the middle of the sea.
In a troubled calm he listens to them sing:
    Stop the ship! Listen to two Sirens
with voices sweet as honey;
anyone that passes us in the black ship
and does not stop to listen to our song
is sailing on without learning anything;
for we know everything that happens
on earth to every single person!
    They helped him to think again of Circe
who craved only what is beautiful: to know everything.

gl'invidiasse ciò che solo è bello:
saper le cose. E ciò dovea la Maga
dalle molt'erbe, in mezzo alle sue belve.
Ma l'uomo eretto, ch'ha il pensier dal cielo,
dovea fermarsi, udire, anche se l'ossa
aveano poi da biancheggiar nel prato,
e raggrinzarsi intorno lor la pelle.
Passare ei non doveva oltre, se anco
gli si vietava riveder la moglie
e il caro figlio e la sua patria terra.
E ai vecchi curvi il vecchio Eroe parlò:
Uomini, andiamo a ciò che solo è bene:
a udire il canto delle due Sirene.
Io voglio udirlo, eretto su la nave,
né già legato con le funi ignave:
libero! alzando su la ciurma anela
la testa bianca come bianca vela;
e tutto quanto nella terra avviene
saper dal labbro delle due Sirene.
Disse, e ne punse ai remiganti il cuore,
che seduti coi remi battean l'acqua,
saper volendo ciò che avviene in terra:
se avea fruttato la sassosa vigna,
se la vacca avea fatto, se il vicino
aveva d'orzo più raccolto o meno,
e che facea la fida moglie allora,
se andava al fonte, se filava in casa.

And there was the witch with many herbs,
with her wild animals all around her.
But the enlightened man, whose thoughts come from
the sky above, can stop, can hear, even if
his bones have turned as white as the meadows,
and the skin wrinkles around them.
He must pass through where no one has gone, or else
he is forbidden to see his wife again
and his dear son and his native country.
    To the old crew bent over their oars the old hero says:
"Men, we are going to do the only thing that is good,
to hear the songs of the two sirens.
I want to hear them standing up on the deck,
not tied, as before, with cowardly ropes:
free! Raising my head above the crew,
holding it up like the white sail; to know
everything on earth that happens,
to know it from the lips of the two Sirens."
    He said it, and the oarsmen seemed struck to the heart
they sat among the oars cutting the water,
wanting to know all that happens on earth:
if the rocky vineyard has borne fruit,
if the cow has grown up, if the neighbor
has harvested more barley or less,
what the faithful wife does,
if she goes to the spring, if she spins in the house.

XXII. In cammino

Ed ecco giunse all'isola dei loti.
E sedean sulla riva uomini e donne,
sazi di loto, in dolce oblìo composti.
E sorsero, ai canuti remiganti
offrendo pii la floreal vivanda.
O così vecchi erranti per il mare,
mangiate il miele dell'oblìo ch'è tempo!
Passò la nave, e lento per il cielo
il sonnolento lor grido vanì.
E quindi venne all'isola dei sassi.
E su le rupi stavano i giganti,
come in vedetta, e su la nave urlando
piovean pietre da carico con alto
fracasso. A stento si salvò la nave.
E quindi giunse all'isola dei morti.
E giacean lungo il fiume uomini e donne,
sazi di vita, sotto i salci e i pioppi.
Volsero il capo; e videro quei vecchi;
e alcuno il figlio ravvisò fra loro,
più di lui vecchio, e per pietà di loro
gemean: Venite a riposare: è tempo!
Passò la nave, ed esile sul mare
il loro morto mormorio vanì.
E di lì venne all'isola del sole.
E pascean per i prati le giovenche
candide e nere, con le dee custodi.
Essi udiano mugliare nella luce
dorata. A stento lontanò la nave.

XXII. Along the Way

And now he came to the island of lotuses.
And there were men and women sitting along
the shore, sated with lotus in a state
of sweet oblivion. And they rose, offering
the faithful old oarsmen that flower as food.
"O, men wandering the seas, it is time,
now for you to eat the honey of oblivion."
The ship passes and their sleepy cries vanish
softly through the forgetful skies.
      And so they arrive at the stone island
of the Lestrygonians. And on its cliffs were giants
placed as sentinels and they rained heavy rocks down
onto the ship, which shattered with a great crash.
      And the ship goes on to the island of the dead.
And women and men lay around the banks of
the ocean's river, sated with life, under willows
and poplars. They looked and saw on the ship
sons older than themselves and then,
moved by pity for the oarsmen, moaned:
"Come and take your rest: it is time!"
The ship had barely passed on when
the lifeless murmuring disappeared.
      And then it came to the island of the sun.
And the young bulls, black ones and white ones,
grazed in the pastures, tended by goddesses;
the men heard the cattle lowing in the golden
light; and with great effort they steered the ship clear.

E di lì giunse all'isola del vento.
E sopra il muro d'infrangibil bronzo
vide i sei figli e le sei figlie a guardia.
E videro la nave, essi, e nel bianco
suo timoniere, parso in prima un cigno
o una cicogna, uno Odisseo conobbe,
che così vecchio anco sfidava i venti;
e con un solo sibilo sul vecchio
scesero insieme di sul liscio masso.
Ed ora l'ira li portò, dei venti,
per giorni e notti, e li sospinse verso
le rupi erranti, ma così veloce,
che a mezzo un cozzo delle rupi dure
come uno strale scivolò la nave.
E allora l'aspra raffica discorde
portava lei contro Cariddi e Scilla.
E già l'Eroe sentì Scilla abbaiare,
come inquïeto cucciolo alla luna,
sentì Cariddi brontolar bollendo,
come il lebete ad una molta fiamma;
e le dodici branche avventò Scilla,
ed assorbì la salsa acqua Cariddi:
invano. Era passata oltre la nave.
E tornarono i venti alla lor casa
cinta di bronzo, mormorando cupi
tra loro, in rissa. E venne un'alta calma
senza il più lieve soffio, e sopra il mare
un dio forse era, che addormentò l'onde.

And they arrived at Aeolus's island of the wind.
On top of a wall of impenetrable bronze he
saw a guard of seven sons and seven daughters,
and they saw the ship, and in the light,
its pilot appeared at first to be a swan
or a stork, but one of them recognized Odysseus,
who was old enough to defy the winds,
and with just one whistle they descended
from the slippery rocks to the old hero.
And now the angry winds carried them forward,
for days and nights, toward the wandering cliffs,
where they arrived so abruptly that they almost
smashed against those sharp and treacherous rocks,
but then slipped through like a swift arrow.

And then a violent change of wind threw them
against Charybdis and Scylla. And now the hero
heard Scylla yelping like a nervous dog
howling at the moon and he heard the rumbling
boil of Charybdis, like a cauldron on a raging fire;
and the twelve arms of Scylla menaced them and
Charybdis gulped down the salty water: in vain.
The ship had already passed on through.

And the winds turned around toward
their home, surrounded by bronze, muttering
darkly among themselves, in anger. And the ship
came into a deep calm without the slightest breeze,
breathless, and perhaps there was some god who
hovered over the sea and lulled the waves to sleep.

XXIII. IL VERO

Ed il prato fiorito era nel mare,
nel mare liscio come un cielo; e il canto
non risonava delle due Sirene,
ancora, perché il prato era lontano.
E il vecchio Eroe sentì che una sommessa
forza, corrente sotto il mare calmo,
spingea la nave verso le Sirene
e disse agli altri d'inalzare i remi:
La nave corre ora da sé, compagni!
Non turbi il rombo del remeggio i canti
delle Sirene. Ormai le udremo. Il canto
placidi udite, il braccio su lo scalmo.
E la corrente tacita e soave
più sempre avanti sospingea la nave.
E il divino Odisseo vide alla punta
dell'isola fiorita le Sirene,
stese tra i fiori, con il capo eretto
su gli ozïosi cubiti, guardando
il mare calmo avanti sé, guardando
il roseo sole che sorgea di contro;
guardando immote; e la lor ombra lunga
dietro rigava l'isola dei fiori.
Dormite? L'alba già passò. Già gli occhi
vi cerca il sole tra le ciglia molli.
Sirene, io sono ancora quel mortale
che v'ascoltò, ma non poté sostare.
E la corrente tacita e soave
più sempre avanti sospingea la nave.

XXIII. The Truth

And there was a flowering garden in the sea,
in a sea glossy as the sky; and a song
of two Sirens did not resound yet,
because the meadow was distant.
And the old hero felt a strong premonition,
a current running in the calm sea,
pushing the boat toward the Sirens;
and he told the men to raise their oars:
    "The ship turns away from them now, friends!
But don't worry that the roar of the rowing
disturbs the songs of the Sirens. By now
we should hear them. Listen to the song
calmly, your arms on the oarlocks."
And the current running quiet and smooth
pushes the ship forward more and more.
And the godlike Odysseus sees at the top
of the blooming island, the Sirens,
stretched out among the flowers, heads
erect, upright on idle elbows, watching
the rosy sun rising across from them;
watching, motionless; and their long shadows
were stripes across the island of flowers.
    "Are you sleeping? The dawn has passed
already. Already eyes under delicate brows
look for the sun. Sirens, I am still mortal.
I heard you, but I could not stop."
    And the current ran on, quiet and smooth,
pushing the ship forward more and more.

E il vecchio vide che le due Sirene,
le ciglia alzate su le due pupille,
avanti sé miravano, nel sole
fisse, od in lui, nella sua nave nera.
E su la calma immobile del mare,
alta e sicura egli inalzò la voce.
Son io! Son io, che torno per sapere!
Ché molto io vidi, come voi vedete
me. Sì; ma tutto ch'io guardai nel mondo,
mi riguardò; mi domandò: Chi sono?
E la corrente rapida e soave
più sempre avanti sospingea la nave.
E il Vecchio vide un grande mucchio d'ossa
d'uomini, e pelli raggrinzate intorno,
presso le due Sirene, immobilmente
stese sul lido, simili a due scogli.
Vedo. Sia pure. Questo duro ossame
cresca quel mucchio. Ma, voi due, parlate!
Ma dite un vero, un solo a me, tra il tutto,
prima ch'io muoia, a ciò ch'io sia vissuto!
E la corrente rapida e soave
più sempre avanti sospingea la nave.
E s'ergean su la nave alte le fronti,
con gli occhi fissi, delle due Sirene.
Solo mi resta un attimo. Vi prego!
Ditemi almeno chi sono io! chi ero!
E tra i due scogli si spezzò la nave.

And the old man sees the two Sirens,
their eyebrows raised high above their pupils,
gazing straight ahead, at the fixed sun,
or at him, in his black ship.
And over the unchanging calm of the sea,
a voice rises from him, deep and sure,
     "I am he! I've returned, to learn!
I am here, as you see me now.
Yes; all that I see in the world
regards me; questions me: asks me what I am."
     And the current ran on, quiet and smooth,
pushing the ship forward more and more.
     And the old man sees a great pile of bones,
men's bones, and shriveled skin near them,
close to the Sirens, stretched out,
motionless, on the shore, like two reefs.
     "I see. Let it be. You may be innocent. But
how much this hard pile of bones
has grown. Speak, you two.
Tell me the truth, to me alone,
of all men, before I doubt that I have lived!"
     And the current ran on, quiet and smooth,
pushing the ship forward more and more.
     And the ship thrust itself high, and above
the brows of the two Sirens while their fixed eyes looked on.
     "I will have but a moment. I beg
you! At least tell me what I am, what I will be."
     And between the two reefs the ship was shattered.

XXIV. Calypso

ascoltala interpretata da Paola Pitagora

E il mare azzurro che l'amò, più oltre
spinse Odisseo, per nove giorni e notti,
e lo sospinse all'isola lontana,
alla spelonca, cui fioriva all'orlo
carica d'uve la pampinea vite.
E fosca intorno le crescea la selva
d'ontani e d'odoriferi cipressi;
e falchi e gufi e garrule cornacchie
v'aveano il nido. E non dei vivi alcuno,
né dio né uomo, vi poneva il piede.
Or tra le foglie della selva i falchi
battean le rumorose ale, e dai buchi
soffiavano, dei vecchi alberi, i gufi,
e dai rami le garrule cornacchie
garrian di cosa che avvenia nel mare.
Ed ella che tessea dentro cantando,
presso la vampa d'olezzante cedro,
stupì, frastuono udendo nella selva,
e in cuore disse: Ahimè, ch'udii la voce
delle cornacchie e il rifiatar dei gufi!
E tra le dense foglie aliano i falchi.
Non forse hanno veduto a fior dell'onda
un qualche dio, che come un grande smergo
viene sui gorghi sterili del mare?
O muove già senz'orma come il vento,
sui prati molli di viola e d'appio?
Ma mi sia lungi dall'orecchio il detto!
In odio hanno gli dei la solitaria

XXIV. Calypso

And the blue sea loved him, swept him
far out for nine days and nights,
swept him to a distant island,
to the cave covered with leaves
of grape vines blooming to the edge.
And around it, a gloomy forest
of alders and pungent cypresses;
and hawks and owls and squawking crows
making their nests there. And nothing left alive,
neither god nor man, ever stepped there.
Then, among the leaves of the forest, the hawks
beat their noisy wings, chasing out
the owls from holes in the old trees,
and from branches, the squawking crows
flapped at the thing that came from the sea.
And Calypso wove a song inside herself,
near the fragrant blaze of a cedar,
astonished, hearing an uproar in the forest,
and, in her heart, said: "Oh, I heard omens,
the voice of the crow and the hoot of the owl!
And among the dense leaves the hawks are fluttering.
Is it because they have seen, on the crest of a wave,
some god, who, like a huge cormorant, dives through
the impossible whirlpools of the sea?
Or moves without footsteps, like the wind, over
the soft meadow of violets and white flowers?
But it seems too far away for me to hear.
There's a hatred the gods have for solitary

Nasconditrice. E ben lo so, da quando
l'uomo che amavo, rimandai sul mare
al suo dolore. O che vedete, o gufi
dagli occhi tondi, e garrule cornacchie?
Ed ecco usciva con la spola in mano,
d'oro, e guardò. Giaceva in terra, fuori
del mare, al piè della spelonca, un uomo,
sommosso ancor dall'ultima onda: e il bianco
capo accennava di saper quell'antro,
tremando un poco; e sopra l'uomo un tralcio
pendea con lunghi grappoli dell'uve.
Era Odisseo: lo riportava il mare
alla sua dea: lo riportava morto
alla Nasconditrice solitaria,
all'isola deserta che frondeggia
nell'ombelico dell'eterno mare.
Nudo tornava chi rigò di pianto
le vesti eterne che la dea gli dava;
bianco e tremante nella morte ancora,
chi l'immortale gioventù non volle.
Ed ella avvolse l'uomo nella nube
dei suoi capelli; ed ululò sul flutto
sterile, dove non l'udia nessuno:
- Non esser mai! non esser mai! più nulla,
ma meno morte, che non esser più! -

Calypso. And I know it well, from when
I sent the man I loved back to the sea
to his sadness. O can you see, owl
with your round eyes, and you, squawking crows?"
    And so she left, gold spool in hand,
and kept watch. He lay on the earth, beyond
the sea, at the foot of the cave, just a man, sleeping
on the last journey's wave: and he, white-headed,
knew that cave of hers very well,
and above him a vine shoot, trembling
a little, hung with long clusters of grapes.
    It was Odysseus: the sea returned him
to his goddess: it brought him back dead
to the solitary Calypso, to the deserted island
that branched out from the navel of the eternal sea.
Naked, he returned, who once was clothed in garments
of plants the eternal goddess gave him;
white and trembling in death, he who once
wore the immortality of his youth.
    And she wrapped the hero in a cloud
of her hair, and she howled across the arid
waves where no one could hear:
"Not to be! Not to be! More than nothing,
but less than dead, not ever to be again."

Textual Notes

November (*Novembre*) is poem no. XVIII from the sequence *In Compagna* (from *Myricae*).

Lightning (*Il Lampo*) is poem no. IX from the sequence *Tristrezze* (from *Myricae*).

Autumn Diary (*Diario autunnale*) is poem no. II from the sequence by that title (from Canti di Castelvecchio).

Night-blooming Jasmine (*Il gelsomino notturno*) is from *Canti di Castelvecchio*.

Thunderstorm (*Temporale*) is from *Canti di Castelvecchio*.

Passage (*Il transito*) and The Book (*Il libro*) are from the sequence *Il Due Fanciulli–I Due Orfani* (*from Primi Poemetti*).

The Kiss of Death (*Il bacio del morto*) is from *Myricae*.

The Clock at Barga (*L'ora di Barga*) is from *Canti di Castelvecchio*.

A Country Walk (*L'ultima passeggiata*) is from *Myricae*.

August 10 (*X Augusto*) (from *Elegies, III*) is from *Myricae*.

The Courtesan (*L'etera*), Solon, The Sleep of Odysseus and Last Voyage (*L'ultimo viaggio*) are from *Poemi Conviviali*.

For our source text, we used Wikisource, and *Pascoli, Tutti le poesie* (Grandi Tascabili Economici Newton, 2001), Arnaldo Colasanti, editor.

The Translators

DEBORAH BROWN'S forthcoming poetry collection, *Walking the Dog's Shadow*, won the A. Poulin, Jr. Poetry Prize from BOA Editions. She is a professor of English at the University of New Hampshire, Manchester, where she has received the University's Excellence in Teaching Award. She is an editor, with Maxine Kumin and Annie Finch, of *Lofty Dogmas: Poets on Poetics* (University of Arkansas Press, 2005). Her essays, poems and translations have been published in *American Literature*, *Modern Language Studies*, *Prairie Schooner*, *The Alaska Quarterly Review*, *The Women's Review of Books*, *The Connecticut Review* and other literary journals.

RICHARD JACKSON is the author of ten books of poems, most recently *Resonance* (Ashland Poetry Press, 2010), *Half Lives: Petrarchan Poems* (Autumn House, 2004), *Unauthorized Autobiography: New and Selected Poems* (Ashland, 2003), *Heartwall* (University of Massachusetts, 2000 Juniper Prize), and *Svetovi Narazen* (Slovenia, 2001). His own poems have been translated into fifteen languages. He has edited two anthologies of Slovene poetry, the *Selected Poems of Iztok Osojnik* (Slovenia), and *Poetry Miscellany*. In 2000, he was awarded the Order of Freedom Medal for literary and humanitarian work in the Balkans by the President of Slovenia and has received a Guggenheim, NEA, NEH, two Witter-Bynner and Fulbright Fellowships, and five Pushcart Prizes. He has won two teaching awards at UT-Chattanooga and the Vermont College MFA program. His previous book of translation is Alexander Persolja's, *Potovanje Sonca, (Journey of the Sun)* from Slovene, 2008.

SUSAN THOMAS has stories, poems and translations in many journals and anthologies and has won the Iowa Poetry Award from Iowa Review, the Ann Stanford Prize from University of Southern California, and the 2010 MR Prize from the Mississippi Review. Her collection, *State of Blessed Gluttony*, (Red Hen Press, 2004), won the Benjamin Saltman Prize. She is also the author of two chapbooks, *The Hand Waves Goodbye*, and *Voice of the Empty Notebook*.